Contents

CONTENTS

Lemon Syrup Madeira Cake

This cake is soaked in lemon syrup so stays moist and is infused with tangy citrus flavour.

ingredients

SERVES TEN

- 250g/9oz/1 cup plus 2 tbsp butter, softened
- 225g/8oz/generous 1 cup caster (superfine) sugar
- 5 eggs
- 275g/10oz/2½ cups plain (all-purpose) flour, sifted
- 10ml/2 tsp baking powder
- pinch of salt

For the sugar crust
- 60ml/4 tbsp freshly squeezed lemon juice
- 15ml/1 tbsp golden (light corn) syrup
- 30ml/2 tbsp sugar

1 Preheat the oven to 180°C/350°F/Gas 4. Lightly grease a 1kg/2¼lb loaf tin (pan).

2 In a large glass bowl, beat the butter and sugar together until the mixture is light and creamy, then gradually beat in the eggs.

cook's tip

Make double the quantity. Omit the syrup from one and leave it plain. Cool, then freeze to use at a later date.

3 Mix together the sifted flour, baking powder and salt, and fold in gently.

4 Spoon the mixture carefully into the prepared tin, level the top with the back of a spoon and bake for 1¼ hours, or until a skewer pushed into the middle of the cake comes out clean.

5 Remove the cake from the oven and, while it is still warm and in the tin, use a skewer to pierce it several times right the way through.

6 Warm together the lemon juice and syrup, add the sugar and immediately spoon over the cake, so the flavoured syrup soaks through but leaves some sugar crystals on the top. Chill the cake for several hours or overnight before serving.

NUTRITIONAL INFORMATION: Energy 422kcal/1764kJ; Protein 6g; Carbohydrate 49.4g, of which sugars 28.4g; Fat 23.7g, of which saturates 13.9g; Cholesterol 148mg; Calcium 71mg; Fibre 0.9g; Sodium 193mg.

One-stage Victoria Sandwich

This simple recipe for the classic Victoria sandwich will always go down a treat.

ingredients

MAKES ONE 18cm/7in
ROUND CAKE

- 175g/6oz/1½ cups self-raising (self-rising) flour
- pinch of salt
- 175g/6oz/¾ cup butter, softened
- 175g/6oz/scant 1 cup caster (superfine) sugar
- 3 eggs
- 300ml/½ pint/1¼ cups double (heavy) cream or 225g/8oz/1 cup cream cheese or low-fat soft cheese
- 60–90ml/4–6 tbsp raspberry jam
- caster (superfine) sugar or icing (confectioners') sugar

1 Preheat the oven to 180°C/350°F/Gas 4. Lightly grease two 18cm/7in shallow round cake tins (pans), line the bases with baking parchment and grease the paper.

variation

Whip 300ml/½ pint/1¼ cups double (heavy) cream with 5ml/1 tsp icing (confectioners') sugar until stiff. Halve 450g/1lb/4 cups strawberries. Use half of the cream and fruit as a filling, and the rest on top.

2 Put the flour, salt, butter, caster sugar and eggs into a large bowl. Whisk the ingredients together until smooth and creamy.

3 Divide the mixture equally between the two prepared cake tins and carefully smooth out the surfaces with the back of a spoon.

4 Bake in the oven for about 25–30 minutes, or until a skewer inserted into the centre of each cake comes out clean.

5 Carefully turn the two cakes out on to a wire rack, then peel off the paper and allow to cool.

6 Whip the cream in a bowl until soft peaks form or beat the cheese lightly

7 Place one of the cakes on to a serving plate and spread with the raspberry jam and cream or soft cheese. Place the other cake on top.

8 Dredge the top of the cake with icing sugar.

NUTRITIONAL INFORMATION: Energy 2965kcal/12419kJ; Protein 37.5g; Carbohydrate 361.3g, of which sugars 227.9g; Fat 162.8g, of which saturates 96.2g; Cholesterol 944mg; Calcium 462mg; Fibre 5.4g; Sodium 130mg.

Really Sticky Ginger Cake

The secret of this cake's dark, rich stickiness lies in the generous amount of treacle used.

ingredients

MAKES ONE 18cm/7in
SQUARE CAKE

- 225g/8oz/2 cups plain (all-purpose) flour
- 10ml/2 tsp ground ginger
- 5ml/1 tsp mixed (apple pie) spice
- pinch of salt
- 2 pieces stem (preserved) ginger, drained and chopped
- 115g/4oz/½ cup butter, softened
- 115g/4oz/⅔ cup dark muscovado (molasses) sugar, sifted
- 275g/10oz/scant 1 cup black treacle or molasses, at room temperature
- 2 eggs, beaten
- 2.5ml/½ tsp bicarbonate of soda (baking soda)
- 30ml/2 tbsp milk, warmed
- butter or cream cheese, to serve

1 Preheat the oven to 160°C/325°F/Gas 3. Grease and line an 18cm/7in square cake tin (pan).

2 Sift the flour, ground ginger, mixed spice and salt together. Add the stem ginger, tossing it in the flour thoroughly.

3 Cream the butter and sugar together until fluffy, then gradually beat in the treacle or molasses. Gradually beat in the eggs, then the flour mixture. Dissolve the bicarbonate of soda in the milk and gradually beat this into the mixture.

4 Pour the mixture into the tin, teasing it into the corners, and bake for 45 minutes.

5 Reduce the oven temperature to 150°C/300°F/Gas 2 and bake for a further 30 minutes, until a metal skewer inserted into the middle of the cake comes out clean. It should look very dark and slightly risen. Don't worry if the cake sinks slightly in the middle.

6 Cool for 5 minutes in the tin, then turn out and cool completely on a wire rack.

7 At this stage, the ginger cake will be dark, but not sticky at all. Keep it for two to three days in an airtight container and the outside will become wonderfully sticky and moist.

8 When ready, slice the cake and serve spread with butter or cream cheese.

NUTRITIONAL INFORMATION: Energy 2987kcal/12579kJ; Protein 41.5g; Carbohydrate 487.1g, of which sugars 309.4g; Fat 111g, of which saturates 64.1g; Cholesterol 628mg; Calcium 2029mg; Fibre 7g; Sodium 1364mg.

Banana Bread

The bananas in this cake make it lovely and moist. Serve spread with butter for afternoon tea.

ingredients

MAKES ONE 21 x 12cm/8½ x 4½in LOAF

- 200g/7oz/1¾ cups plain (all-purpose) flour
- 11.5ml/2¼ tsp baking powder
- 2.5ml/½ tsp salt
- 4ml/¾ tsp ground cinnamon (optional)
- 60ml/4 tbsp wheatgerm
- 65g/2½oz/5 tbsp butter, at room temperature
- 115g/4oz/generous ½ cup caster (superfine) sugar
- 4ml/¾ tsp grated lemon rind
- 3 ripe bananas, mashed until smooth
- 2 eggs, beaten

1 Preheat the oven to 180°C/ 350°F/Gas 4. Lightly grease and flour a 21 x 12cm/8½ x 4½in loaf tin (pan).

2 Sift together the flour, baking powder, salt and cinnamon, if using, into a large bowl. Stir in the wheatgerm.

3 In another bowl, combine the butter with the caster sugar and the grated lemon rind. Beat the ingredients thoroughly with a wooden spoon until the mixture is light and fluffy.

4 Add the mashed bananas and eggs, and mix. Add the dry ingredients and blend evenly.

5 Spoon into the loaf tin. Bake for 50–60 minutes, or until a skewer inserted into the centre comes out clean.

6 Cool the bread in the tin for about 5 minutes, then turn out on to a wire rack and allow to cool completely.

7 Serve the banana bread sliced, spread with butter.

cook's tip

Wheatgerm is the heart of the wheat grain and contains many nutrients and vitamins. It must always be used fresh and should be stored in an airtight container.

NUTRITIONAL INFORMATION: Energy 2265kcal/9548kJ; Protein 51.9g; Carbohydrate 372.4g, of which sugars 195.9g; Fat 73.6g, of which saturates 38.4g; Cholesterol 519mg; Calcium 461mg; Fibre 18.9g; Sodium 553mg.

Pecan Cake

Serve this cake with whipped cream or crème fraîche. Redcurrants add a splash of colour.

ingredients

SERVES EIGHT TO TEN

- 115g/4oz/1 cup pecan nuts
- 115g/4oz/½ cup butter
- 115g/4oz/½ cup soft light brown sugar
- 5ml/1 tsp vanilla extract
- 4 large eggs, separated
- 75g/3oz/¾ cup plain (all-purpose) flour
- pinch of salt
- 12 whole pecan nuts
- whipped cream or crème fraîche, to serve

For drizzling

- 50g/2oz/¼ cup butter
- 120ml/4fl oz/scant ½ cup clear honey

1 Preheat the oven to 180°C/350°F/Gas 4. Grease a 20cm/8in round spring-form cake tin (pan). Toast the pecan nuts in a dry frying pan for 5 minutes, shaking frequently. Grind finely in a blender or food processor. Place in a bowl.

2 Cream the butter with the sugar, then beat in the vanilla extract and egg yolks.

3 Add the flour to the ground nuts and mix. Whisk the egg whites with the salt in a bowl until soft peaks form.

4 Fold the egg whites into the butter mixture, then fold in the flour and nut mixture.

5 Spoon the mixture into the prepared cake tin and bake for 30 minutes, or until a skewer inserted into the centre comes out clean. Remove from the oven.

6 Allow the pecan cake to cool slightly in the tin for about 5 minutes, then remove the sides of the tin and stand the cake on a wire rack until it has cooled down completely.

7 Arrange the pecans on top of the cake. Transfer to a plate.

8 Melt the butter in a small pan, add the honey and bring to the boil, stirring. Simmer gently for 3 minutes. Pour over the cake and serve.

NUTRITIONAL INFORMATION: Energy 428kcal/1785kJ; Protein 6.2g; Carbohydrate 34.7g, of which sugars 27.4g; Fat 30.5g, of which saturates 12.5g; Cholesterol 158mg; Calcium 51mg; Fibre 1g; Sodium 170mg.

Iced Angel Cake

Served with fromage frais or low-fat yogurt and fresh raspberries, this makes a light teatime treat.

ingredients

SERVES TEN

- 40g/1½oz/scant ½ cup cornflour (cornstarch)
- 40g/1½oz/scant ½ cup plain all-purpose) flour
- 8 egg whites
- 225g/8oz/generous 1 cup caster (superfine) sugar, plus extra for sprinkling
- 5ml/1 tsp vanilla extract
- icing (confectioners') sugar, for dusting

cook's tip

This cake can also be made in a 20cm/8in round cake tin (pan).

1 Preheat the oven to 180°C/350°F/Gas 4. Sift the cornflour and the plain flour together into a bowl. Whisk the egg whites in a large grease-free bowl until very stiff.

variation

Make lemon icing by mixing 175g/6oz/1½ cups icing (confectioners') sugar with 15–30ml/1–2 tbsp lemon juice. Drizzle the icing over the cake and decorate the top with physalis.

2 Gradually add the caster (superfine) sugar and vanilla extract to the egg whites, a spoonful of sugar at a time, whisking until the mixture is thick and glossy.

3 Fold the flour mixture into the sugar and egg whites with a large metal spoon.

4 Spoon the cake mixture into an ungreased 25cm/10in angel cake tin (pan), smooth over the surface with the back of a spoon and bake in the oven for 40–45 minutes.

5 Sprinkle a piece of baking parchment with caster sugar and set an egg cup in the centre. Invert the cake tin over the paper, balancing the cake on the egg cup. When cold, the cake will drop out of the tin. Dust with icing sugar and serve.

NUTRITIONAL INFORMATION: Energy 178kcal/762kJ; Protein 4.3g; Carbohydrate 42.6g, of which sugars 30g; Fat 0.2g, of which saturates 0g; Cholesterol 0mg; Calcium 35.4mg; Fibre 0.4g; Sodium 64.5mg.

Dundee Cake

A classic Scottish fruit cake, this is made with mixed peel, dried fruit, almonds and spices.

ingredients

SERVES SIXTEEN TO TWENTY

- 175g/6oz/¾ cup butter
- 175g/6oz/¾ cup soft light brown sugar
- 3 eggs
- 225g/8oz/2 cups plain (all-purpose) flour
- 10ml/2 tsp baking powder
- 5ml/1 tsp ground cinnamon
- 2.5ml/½ tsp ground cloves
- 1.5ml/¼ tsp freshly grated nutmeg
- 225g/8oz/generous 1½ cups sultanas (golden raisins)
- 175g/6oz/¾ cup glacé (candied) cherries
- 115g/4oz/⅔ cup mixed chopped (candied) peel
- 50g/2oz/½ cup blanched almonds, roughly chopped
- grated rind of 1 lemon
- 30ml/2 tbsp brandy
- 75g/3oz/¾ cup whole blanched almonds, to decorate

1 Preheat the oven to 160°C/325°F/Gas 3. Grease and line a 20cm/8in round, deep cake tin (pan).

2 Cream the butter and sugar together in a mixing bowl. Add the eggs, one at a time, beating thoroughly after each addition.

3 Sift the flour, baking powder and spices together in a large bowl. Fold these into the creamed mixture alternately with the remaining ingredients, apart from the whole almonds. Mix together thoroughly until evenly blended.

4 Carefully transfer the mixture to the prepared cake tin and smooth the surface, making a dip in the centre.

5 Decorate the top by pressing the almonds in decreasing circles over the entire surface.

6 Bake in the preheated oven for 2–2¼ hours, until a skewer inserted into the centre comes out clean.

7 Cool in the tin for 30 minutes, then transfer to a wire rack to cool fully.

cook's tip

Fruit cakes improve in flavour if left in a cool place for up to 3 months. Wrap in baking parchment and a layer of foil.

NUTRITIONAL INFORMATION: Energy 321kcal/1347kJ; Protein 4.7g; Carbohydrate 44.2g, of which sugars 33.3g; Fat 14.7g, of which saturates 6.4g; Cholesterol 59mg; Calcium 76mg; Fibre 1.7g; Sodium 107mg.

Fresh Apricot Cake

Almonds are perfect partners for fresh apricots, and this is a great way to use firm fruits.

ingredients

MAKES EIGHT SLICES

- 175g/6oz/1½ cups self-raising (self-rising) flour
- 175g/6oz/¾ cup butter
- 175g/6oz/¾ cup caster (superfine) sugar
- 115g/4oz/1 cup ground almonds
- 3 eggs
- 5ml/1 tsp almond extract
- 2.5ml/½ tsp baking powder
- 8 apricots

For the topping

- 30ml/2 tbsp demerara (raw) sugar
- 50g/2oz/½ cup slivered almonds

1 Preheat the oven to 160°C/ 325°F/Gas 3. Grease an 18cm/ 7in round cake tin (pan) and line with baking parchment.

2 Put all the ingredients, except the apricots, in a bowl and whisk until creamy.

3 Stone (pit) the apricots and chop the flesh. Gradually fold the chopped apricots into the cake mixture, then spoon into the prepared cake tin.

4 Make a hollow in the centre of the cake mixture with the back of a spoon, then scatter 15ml/1 tbsp of the demerara sugar over for the topping, with the slivered almonds.

5 Bake for about 1½ hours, or until a metal skewer inserted into the middle of the cake comes out clean.

6 Scatter the remaining demerara sugar over the top of the cake and leave to cool for about 10 minutes in the tin.

7 Remove from the tin, peel off the paper and finish cooling on a wire rack.

cook's tip

For a special treat, serve warm. Drizzle with Cointreau, Grand Marnier or other orange liqueur before serving with ice cream.

NUTRITIONAL INFORMATION: Energy 506kcal/2115kJ; Protein 9.4g; Carbohydrate 48.6g, of which sugars 31.4g; Fat 31.9g, of which saturates 12.9g; Cholesterol 118mg; Calcium 115mg; Fibre 3g; Sodium 165mg.

Apple Cake

This moist cake is perhaps best in autumn, when home-grown apples are in season.

ingredients

MAKES ONE 20cm/8in CAKE

- 225g/8oz/2 cups self-raising (self-rising) flour
- good pinch of salt
- pinch of ground cloves or mixed (apple pie) spice
- 115g/4oz/½ cup butter, at room temperature or softened
- 3 or 4 cooking apples, such as Bramley's Seedling
- 115g/4oz/generous ½ cup caster (superfine) sugar
- 2 eggs, beaten
- a little milk to mix
- granulated (white) sugar to sprinkle over

1 Preheat the oven to 190°C/375°F/Gas 5 and butter a 20cm/8in cake tin (pan).

2 Sieve the flour, salt and ground cloves or mixed spice together into a large bowl.

3 Cut in the butter and rub into the mixture until it resembles fine breadcrumbs.

4 Carefully peel and core the apples. Slice them thinly using a sharp knife and add to the rubbed-in mixture with the caster sugar.

5 Mix in the eggs and enough milk to make a fairly stiff dough.

6 Turn the apple mixture into the prepared cake tin, spreading it down evenly with the back of a spoon. Sprinkle the top with granulated sugar.

7 Bake in the preheated oven for 30–40 minutes, or until springy to the touch.

8 Allow the apple cake to cool on a wire rack. When cold store in an airtight tin until ready to serve.

cook's tip

Dessert or eating apples do not break down as easily as cooking apples. They are not as tangy and do not have as good a flavour when cooked.

NUTRITIONAL INFORMATION: Energy 2315kcal/9717kJ; Protein 37g; Carbohydrate 312.5g, of which sugars 145.3g; Fat 110.9g, of which saturates 64.1g; Cholesterol 702mg; Calcium 948mg; Fibre 10.7g; Sodium 1.68g.

Geranium Carrot Cake

The geranium-scented cheese topping makes this carrot cake extra special.

ingredients

MAKES ONE 23 x 12cm/9 x 5in CAKE

- 115g/4oz/1 cup self-raising (self-rising) flour
- 5ml/1 tsp bicarbonate of soda (baking soda)
- 2.5ml/½ tsp ground cinnamon
- 2.5ml/½ tsp ground cloves
- 200g/7oz/scant 1 cup soft light brown sugar
- 225g/8oz/generous 1½ cups grated carrot
- 150g/5oz/scant 1 cup sultanas (golden raisins)
- 150g/5oz/½ cup preserved stem ginger, chopped
- 150g/5oz/scant 1 cup pecan nuts
- 150ml/¼ pint/⅔ cup sunflower oil
- 2 eggs, lightly beaten

For the topping

- 2 or 3 lemon-scented geranium leaves, torn into pieces
- 225g/8oz/2 cups icing (confectioners') sugar
- 50g/2¼oz/generous 4 tbsp cream cheese
- 30g/1¼oz/generous 2 tbsp softened butter
- 5ml/1 tsp grated lemon rind

1 For the topping, put the geranium leaves in a bowl and mix with the icing sugar. Leave in a warm place overnight for the sugar to take up the scent.

2 Preheat the oven to 180°C/350°F/Gas 4. Grease a 23 x 13cm/9 x 5in loaf tin (pan), line the base with baking parchment, and grease the paper.

3 Sift the flour, bicarbonate of soda and spices together. Add the sugar, grated carrots, sultanas, preserved stem ginger and pecan nuts.

4 Stir well, then add the oil and beaten eggs. Mix with an electric mixer for 5 minutes. Pour into the tin and bake for 1 hour. Remove from the oven, leave to stand for a few minutes, and then cool on a wire rack.

5 Make the topping. Remove the pieces of leaf from the icing sugar and discard. Place the cream cheese, butter and lemon rind in a bowl. Using an electric mixer, gradually add the icing sugar, beating until smooth. Spread over the top of the cooled cake.

NUTRITIONAL INFORMATION: Energy 5413kcal/22706kJ; Protein 47.4g; Carbohydrate 740.3g, of which sugars 649.3g; Fat 272.2g, of which saturates 57.5g; Cholesterol 502mg; Calcium 789mg; Fibre 21.4g; Sodium 624mg.

Old-fashioned Treacle Cake

Just a little treacle gives this economical light fruit cake its rich colour and fuller flavour.

ingredients

MAKES A 20cm/8in CAKE

- 250g/9oz/2 cups self-raising (self-rising) flour
- 2.5ml/½ tsp mixed (apple pie) spice
- 75g/3oz/6 tbsp butter, cut into small cubes
- 35g/1oz/2 tbsp caster (superfine) sugar
- 150g/5oz/1 cup mixed dried fruit or a mixture of currants, raisins and sultanas (golden raisins)
- 1 egg
- 15ml/1 tbsp black treacle (molasses)
- 100ml/3½fl oz/scant ½ cup milk

1 Preheat the oven to 180°C/350°F/Gas 5. Butter a shallow 20–23cm/8–9in ovenproof flan dish or baking tin (pan).

2 Sift the flour and spice into a large mixing bowl. Add the butter and, with your fingertips, rub it into the flour until the mixture resembles fine crumbs.

cook's tip

Vary the fruit – use chopped ready-to-eat dried apricots or preserved stem ginger.

3 Stir the sugar and mixed dried fruit into the rubbed-in flour mixture.

4 Beat the egg and, with a small whisk or a fork, stir in the treacle and then the milk. Stir the liquid into the flour to make a fairly stiff but moist consistency, adding a little extra milk if necessary.

5 Carefully transfer the cake mixture to the prepared dish or tin and smooth out the surface evenly with the back of a spoon.

6 Bake for about 1 hour, until the cake has risen, is firm and springy to the touch and fully cooked through. To check if the cake is cooked in the middle, insert a clean metal skewer into the centre – it should come out free of sticky mixture. If the skewer is sticky, replace the cake in the oven and check again with a clean skewer after a further 5 minutes' baking.

7 Leave the cooked treacle cake to cool down completely. Serve it, cut into wedges, straight from the dish.

NUTRITIONAL INFORMATION: Energy 2089kcal/8805kJ; Protein 37.4g; Carbohydrate 343g, of which sugars 152.4g; Fat 72.8g, of which saturates 42.2g; Cholesterol 356mg; Calcium 720mg; Fibre 11.1g; Sodium 676mg.

Choc-orange Battenberg

This attractively presented geometric cake makes a tasty, bitesize afternoon snack.

ingredients

SERVES EIGHT

- 115g/4oz/½ cup margarine
- 115g/4oz/½ cup caster (superfine) sugar
- 2 eggs, beaten
- few drops of vanilla extract
- 115g/4oz/1 cup ground almonds
- 115g/4oz/1 cup self-raising (self-rising) flour, sifted
- grated rind and juice of ½ orange
- 30ml/2 tbsp unsweetened cocoa powder
- 30–45ml/2–3 tbsp milk
- 1 jar chocolate and nut spread
- cornflour (cornstarch), to dust
- 225g/8oz white almond paste

1 Preheat the oven to 180°C/350°F/Gas 4. Grease and line an 18cm/7in square cake tin (pan). Place a double piece of foil across the middle of the tin, to divide it into two equal rectangles.

2 Cream the margarine and sugar in a bowl, then beat in the eggs, vanilla extract and ground almonds. Divide the mixture between two bowls. Fold half the flour into one bowl, then stir in the orange rind and enough juice to give a soft dropping consistency. Set aside.

3 Fold the rest of the flour and cocoa into the remaining bowl of mixture, with enough milk to give a soft dropping consistency.

4 Fill one half of the tin with the orange mixture and the second with the chocolate. Bake for 15 minutes, then reduce the heat to 160°C/325°F/Gas 3, and bake for a further 20 minutes, or until the top is just firm.

5 Leave to cool in the tin for a few minutes then turn out on to a board and cut each one into two identical strips. Cool.

6 Using the chocolate and nut spread, sandwich the cakes together, chocolate and orange side by side, then orange and chocolate on top. Spread the sides with more spread.

7 On a board dusted with cornflour, roll out the almond paste to a rectangle 18cm/7in wide and long enough to wrap around the cake.

8 Wrap, joining underneath. Press to seal. Cut into chequered slices to serve.

NUTRITIONAL INFORMATION: Energy 716kcal/2993kJ; Protein 11.5g; Carbohydrate 77.2g, of which sugars 65g; Fat 42.3g, of which saturates 6.9g; Cholesterol 49mg; Calcium 163mg; Fibre 2.9g; Sodium 204mg.

Carrot and Parsnip Cake

The grated carrots and parsnips in this deliciously light and crumbly cake help to keep it moist.

ingredients

SERVES EIGHT TO TEN

- 1 lemon
- 1 orange
- 15ml/1 tbsp caster (superfine) sugar
- 225g/8oz/1 cup butter
- 225g/8oz/1 cup soft light brown sugar
- 4 eggs
- 225g/8oz/1⅔ cups carrot and parsnip, grated
- 115g/4oz/1¼ cups sultanas (golden raisins)
- 225g/8oz/2 cups self-raising (self-rising) wholemeal flour
- 5ml/1 tsp baking powder

For the topping

- 50g/2oz/¼ cup caster (superfine) sugar
- 1 egg white
- pinch of salt

1 Preheat the oven to 180°C/ 350°F/Gas 4. Grease a 20cm/ 8in loose-based cake tin (pan) and then line the base with baking parchment.

2 Finely grate the lemon and orange. Put half of the rind, selecting the longest shreds, in a bowl and mix with the caster sugar. Arrange the sugar-coated rind on a sheet of baking parchment and leave to dry out.

3 Cream the butter and sugar until fluffy. Add the eggs gradually, then beat well.

4 Stir in the unsugared rinds, grated carrots and parsnips, 30ml/2 tbsp orange juice and the sultanas. Fold in the flour and baking powder, and turn into the prepared tin.

5 Bake for 1½ hours until risen, golden and firm. Leave the cake to cool slightly in the tin, then turn out on to a serving plate.

6 For the topping, place the caster sugar in a bowl over simmering water with 30ml/ 2 tbsp of the orange juice. Stir until the sugar begins to dissolve.

7 Remove from the heat, add the egg white and salt, and whisk for 1 minute with an electric beater. Return to the heat and whisk for 5 minutes until stiff and glossy. Cool slightly, whisking frequently.

8 Swirl the topping over the cake and leave to firm for 1 hour. Sprinkle with the sugared rind.

NUTRITIONAL INFORMATION: Energy 414kcal/1734kJ; Protein 6.2g; Carbohydrate 52.8g, of which sugars 38.9g; Fat 21.3g, of which saturates 12.4g; Cholesterol 124mg; Calcium 47mg; Fibre 2.3g; Sodium 175mg.

Plum Teabread

This sweet and rich bread is good sliced and buttered, toasted or with cheese instead of plain bread.

ingredients

MAKES TWO SMALL LOAVES

- 450g/1lb/4 cups strong white bread flour
- pinch of salt
- 5ml/1 tsp ground cinnamon
- 5ml/1 tsp freshly grated nutmeg
- 12.5ml/2½ tsp easy-blend fast-action yeast granules
- 60ml/4 tbsp soft light brown sugar
- 115g/4oz/3 tbsp butter, diced
- about 100ml/3½fl oz/scant ½ cup milk
- 2 eggs, lightly beaten
- 225g/8oz/1 cup mixed dried fruit, such as raisins and chopped mixed (candied) peel

1 Sift together the flour, salt and spices and then stir in the yeast and sugar. Gently heat the butter and milk until just melted. Add the eggs to the flour and mix well until the mixture can be gathered into a smooth ball of dough.

2 Cover the dough with oiled cling film (plastic wrap) and leave in a warm place for about 1 hour until doubled in size. Grease and line two 450g/1lb loaf tins (pans) with baking parchment and preheat the oven to 190°C/375°F/Gas 5.

3 Knead the dough briefly on a lightly floured surface, working in the dried fruit evenly. Divide between the prepared tins, cover with oiled cling film and leave in a warm place for 30 minutes, or until nearly doubled in size.

4 Cook the loaves for 40 minutes, then turn them out of their tins and return to the hot oven for about 5 minutes or until they sound hollow when tapped on the base. Cool on a wire rack.

cook's tip

Although it is called plum bread, the dough is made with raisins; however, coarsely chopped ready-to-eat stoned (pitted) prunes can be used instead of the raisins.

NUTRITIONAL INFORMATION: Energy 1710kcal/7211kJ; Protein 32.2g; Carbohydrate 285.2g, of which sugars 113.7g; Fat 57.1g, of which saturates 32.5g; Cholesterol 316mg; Calcium 535mg; Fibre 9.1g; Sodium 465mg.

Quick Barm Brack

Barm brack is a traditional Irish fruit cake. If made in loaf tins, it is easier to slice for toasting.

ingredients

MAKES TWO LOAVES

- 450g/1lb/4 cups plain (all-purpose) flour
- 5ml/1 tsp mixed (apple pie) spice
- 2.5ml/½ tsp salt
- 2 sachets easy-blend (rapid-rise) dried yeast
- 75g/3oz/6 tbsp soft dark brown sugar
- 115g/4oz/½ cup butter, melted
- 300ml/½ pint/1¼ cups milk
- 1 egg, lightly beaten
- 375g/13oz/generous 2 cups dried mixed fruit
- 25g/1oz/⅓ cup chopped mixed (candied) peel
- 15ml/1 tbsp caster (superfine) sugar

1 Butter two 450g/1lb loaf tins (pans). Mix the flour, spice, salt, yeast and brown sugar in a large bowl and make a well in the centre.

2 Mix the butter with the milk and lightly beaten egg and add to the bowl.

3 Add the mixed fruit and peel and mix well. Turn the mixture into the loaf tins.

4 Leave the tins in a warm place for about 30 minutes to rise.

5 Meanwhile, preheat the oven to 200°C/400°F/Gas 6.

6 When the dough has doubled in size, bake in the hot oven for about 45 minutes, or until the loaves begin to shrink slightly from the sides of the tins; when turned out and rapped underneath they should sound hollow.

7 Make a glaze for the barm brack by putting the caster sugar in a small measuring jug (cup) with 30ml/2 tbsp boiling water.

8 Remove the loaves from the oven and brush over with the glaze. Return them to the oven for 3 minutes, or until the tops are a rich shiny brown. Turn on to a wire rack to cool.

NUTRITIONAL INFORMATION: Energy 2019kcal/8524kJ; Protein 34.9g; Carbohydrate 364.6g, of which sugars 193.2g; Fat 57g, of which saturates 32.8g; Cholesterol 246mg; Calcium 704mg; Fibre 11.7g; Sodium 590mg.

Sour Cherry Coffee Loaf

Dried sour cherries have a wonderfully concentrated fruit flavour and can be bought in health food shops.

ingredients

SERVES EIGHT

- 175g/6oz/12 tbsp butter
- 175g/6oz/scant 1 cup golden caster (superfine) sugar
- 5ml/1 tsp vanilla extract
- 2 eggs, lightly beaten
- 225g/3oz/2 cups plain (all-purpose) flour
- 1.5ml/¼ tsp baking powder
- 75ml/5 tbsp strong brewed coffee
- 175g/6oz/1 cup dried sour cherries

For the icing

- 50g/2oz/½ cup icing (confectioners') sugar, sifted
- 20ml/4 tsp strong coffee

1 Preheat the oven to 180°C/ 350°F/Gas 4. Grease and line a 900g/2lb loaf tin (pan). Cream the butter, sugar and vanilla until fluffy.

2 Gradually add the eggs, beating continuously.

3 Sift the flour and baking powder together in a small bowl. Fold into the mixture with the coffee and 115g/ 4oz/²/₃ cup of the sour cherries.

4 Carefully transfer the mixture to the prepared tin and level the top with the back of the spoon.

5 Bake in the oven for 1¼ hours, or until the loaf is firm to the touch. Alow to cool in the tin for 5 minutes, then turn out and cool completely on a wire rack.

6 To make the icing, mix together the icing sugar and coffee and the remaining cherries in a bowl.

7 Spoon the icing over the top of the loaf and sides. Leave to set before slicing.

NUTRITIONAL INFORMATION: Energy 307kcal/1282kJ; Protein 2.1g; Carbohydrate 33.1g, of which sugars 33.1g; Fat 19.4g, of which saturates 11.8g; Cholesterol 94mg; Calcium 30mg; Fibre 0.3g; Sodium 152mg.

One-mix Chocolate Sponge

This ridiculously easy recipe produces great results, time after time, with the smallest effort.

ingredients

SERVES EIGHT TO TEN

- 175g/6oz/¾ cup soft margarine
- 115g/4oz/½ cup caster (superfine) sugar
- 60ml/4 tbsp golden (light corn) syrup
- 175g/6oz/1½ cups self-raising (self-rising) flour, sifted
- 30ml/2 tbsp unsweetened cocoa powder, sifted
- 2.5ml/½ tsp salt
- 3 eggs, beaten
- little milk (optional)
- 150ml/¼ pint/⅔ cup whipping cream
- 15–30ml/1–2 tbsp finely shredded marmalade
- icing (confectioners') sugar

1 Preheat the oven to 180°C/ 350°F/Gas 4. Grease two 18cm/ 7in sandwich cake tins (pans).

3 If the cake mixture seems too thick, stir in enough milk to give it a soft dropping consistency.

5 Bake the cakes for about 30 minutes, changing shelves if necessary after 15 minutes, until the tops are just firm and springy to the touch.

6 Leave the cakes to cool for 5 minutes, then remove from the tins and cool on a wire rack.

7 Whip the cream and fold in the marmalade. Use the mixture to sandwich the two cakes together. Sift a little icing sugar over the cake.

2 Cream the margarine, sugar, syrup, flour, cocoa powder, salt and eggs together in a large mixing bowl.

4 Spoon the mixture into the two tins, then smooth the surface with a palette knife or metal spatula.

NUTRITIONAL INFORMATION: Energy 162kcal/675kJ; Protein 13.1g; Carbohydrate 8.5g, of which sugars 7g; Fat 8.6g, of which saturates 3.8g; Cholesterol 44mg; Calcium 42mg; Fibre 3g; Sodium 55mg.

17

Coffee-top Chocolate Cake

This easy all-in-one recipe is a favourite and can be quickly dressed up to make a really special cake.

ingredients

MAKES ONE 18cm/7in ROUND CAKE

- 175g/6oz/1½ cups self-raising (self-rising) flour
- 25ml/1½ tbsp unsweetened cocoa powder
- pinch of salt
- 175g/6oz/¾ cup butter, softened, or easy-spread margarine
- 175g/6oz/¾ cup soft dark brown sugar
- 50g/2oz/½ cup ground almonds
- 3 large (US extra large) eggs, lightly beaten

For the coffee butter icing

- 175g/6oz/¾ cup unsalted (sweet) butter, at warm room temperature
- 350g/12oz/3 cups sifted icing (confectioners') sugar
- 30ml/2 tbsp coffee extract
- whole hazelnuts or pecan nuts to decorate (optional)

1 Preheat the oven to 180°C/350°F/Gas 4 and butter two 18cm/7in diameter sandwich tins (pans).

2 Sift the flour, cocoa powder and salt into a bowl. Cut in the butter or margarine and add the sugar, ground almonds and eggs.

variation

For a deliciously rich touch, add 30ml/2 tbsp of Bailey's Irish Cream to the icing with the coffee extract in stage 5.

3 Mix with a wooden spoon for 2–3 minutes, until thoroughly mixed; the mixture should be smooth, with no traces of butter remaining.

4 Divide the mixture between the prepared tins and bake in the centre of the preheated oven for 25–30 minutes, or until springy to the touch. Turn out and cool on a wire rack.

5 Meanwhile, make the icing: cream the butter well, then gradually beat in the sifted icing sugar and the coffee extract.

6 When the cakes are cold, sandwich together with some of the icing and cover the top and sides with most of the remainder. Pipe the remaining icing around the top in rosettes, and decorate with whole hazelnuts or pecan nuts.

NUTRITIONAL INFORMATION: Energy 5899kcal/24,684kJ; Protein 56.2g; Carbohydrate 691.1g, of which sugars 556.9g; Fat 343.1g, of which saturates 199.7g; Cholesterol 1.43mg; Calcium 1.06mg; Fibre 12.2g; Sodium 3.28mg.

Chocolate Roulade

This ravishing roulade is topped with curls of fresh coconut – perfect for that special occasion.

ingredients

SERVES EIGHT

- 150g/5oz/¾ cup caster (superfine) sugar
- 5 eggs, separated
- 90g/3½oz/scant 1 cup self-raising (self-rising) flour
- 50g/2oz/½ cup unsweetened cocoa powder

For the filling

- 300ml/½ pint/1¼ cups double (heavy) cream
- 45ml/3 tbsp whisky
- 50g/2oz piece solid creamed coconut
- 30ml/2 tbsp caster (superfine) sugar

For the topping

- coarsely grated curls of fresh coconut and chocolate curls

1 Preheat the oven to 180°C/350°F/Gas 4. Grease a 32 x 23cm/13 x 9in Swiss roll tin (jelly roll pan). Dust a sheet of baking parchment with 30ml/2 tbsp of the caster sugar.

2 Place the egg yolks in a bowl. Add the remaining caster sugar and whisk with a hand-held electric mixer until the mixture is thick enough to leave a trail. Sift the flour and cocoa powder over, then fold in evenly.

3 Whisk the egg whites until they form soft peaks.

4 Fold about 15ml/1 tbsp of the whites into the chocolate mixture to lighten it, then fold in the rest evenly.

5 Scrape the mixture into the prepared tin, taking it right into the corners. Smooth the surface with a palette knife, then bake for 20–25 minutes or until well risen and springy to the touch.

6 Turn out on to the sugar-dusted baking parchment and carefully peel off the lining paper. Cover with a damp, clean dish towel and leave to cool.

7 Make the filling. Whisk the cream with the whisky in a bowl until the mixture holds its shape, then finely grate the creamed coconut and stir it in with the sugar.

8 Uncover the sponge and spread three-quarters of the cream mixture to the edges. Roll up carefully from a long side. Transfer to a plate, and pipe or spoon the remaining cream mixture on top. Gently sprinkle the coconut curls on top of the cake with the chocolate curls.

NUTRITIONAL INFORMATION: Energy 394kcal/1640kJ; Protein 6.2g; Carbohydrate 25.3g, of which sugars 24.6g; Fat 29.3g, of which saturates 18g; Cholesterol 170mg; Calcium 58mg; Fibre 0.8g; Sodium 115mg.

Marbled Swiss Roll

Light chocolate sponge and walnut chocolate buttercream provide this twist on a popular recipe.

ingredients

SERVES SIX TO EIGHT

- 90g/3½oz/scant 1 cup plain (all-purpose) flour
- 15ml/1 tbsp unsweetened cocoa powder
- 25g/1oz plain (semisweet) chocolate, grated
- 25g/1oz white chocolate, grated
- 3 eggs
- 115g/4oz/½ cup caster (superfine) sugar
- 30ml/2 tbsp boiling water
- chocolate curls, to decorate

For the filling

- 75g/3oz/6 tbsp unsalted (sweet) butter or margarine
- 175g/6oz/1 cup icing (confectioners') sugar
- 15ml/1 tbsp unsweetened cocoa powder
- 2.5ml/½ tsp vanilla extract
- 45ml/3 tbsp chopped walnuts

1 Preheat the oven to 200°C/400°F/Gas 6. Grease a 30 x 20cm/12 x 8in Swiss roll tin (jelly roll pan) and line with baking parchment.

2 Sift half of the flour with the cocoa powder into a bowl. Stir in the plain chocolate. Sift the rest of the flour into another bowl and stir in the white chocolate.

3 Whisk the eggs and sugar in a bowl over a pan of hot water until smooth. Remove from the heat. Divide equally between two bowls.

4 Fold the white chocolate mixture into one portion, and the plain chocolate mix into the other. Stir 15ml/1 tbsp boiling water into each bowl to soften.

5 Place alternate spoonfuls of the white and chocolate mixtures in the prepared tin and swirl together for a marbled effect. Bake for 15 minutes, or until firm.

6 Turn out on to a sheet of baking parchment. Trim the edges to neaten, cover with a damp, clean dish towel and cool.

7 For the filling, beat together the butter, icing sugar, cocoa powder and vanilla extract until smooth. Mix in the walnuts.

8 Uncover the sponge, lift off the paper and spread the surface with the filling. Roll up from a long side and place on a plate. Decorate with chocolate curls.

NUTRITIONAL INFORMATION: Energy 361kcal/1518kJ; Protein 5.6g; Carbohydrate 51.1g, of which sugars 42g; Fat 16.4g, of which saturates 7.4g; Cholesterol 92mg; Calcium 67mg; Fibre 1.1g; Sodium 125mg.

Citrus Chocolate Angel Cake

Fragrant orange meets luscious chocolate in this delightful cake that is perfect for a special occasion.

ingredients

SERVES TEN

- 25g/1oz/¼ cup plain (all-purpose) flour
- 30ml/2 tbsp unsweetened cocoa powder
- 30ml/2 tbsp cornflour (cornstarch)
- pinch of salt
- 5 egg whites
- 2.5ml/½ tsp cream of tartar
- 115g/4oz/½ cup caster (superfine) sugar
- blanched and shredded rind of 1 orange, to decorate

For the Icing

- 200g/7oz/scant 1 cup caster (superfine) sugar
- 75ml/5 tbsp cold water
- 1 egg white

1 Preheat the oven to 180°C/ 350°F/Gas 4. Sift the flour, cocoa powder, cornflour and salt together three times. Beat the egg whites in a large bowl until foamy. Add the cream of tartar to the egg whites and whisk until soft peaks form.

2 Add the caster sugar to the egg whites a spoonful at a time, whisking after each addition. Add, by sifting, a third of the flour and cocoa mixture, and gently fold in. Repeat, sifting and folding in the flour and cocoa two more times.

3 Spoon the mixture into a 20cm/8in non-stick ring tin (pan) and level the top. Bake for 35 minutes, or until springy when lightly pressed. Turn upside-down on to a wire rack and leave to cool in the tin. Ease the cake out of the tin before making the icing.

4 To make the icing, put the sugar in a pan with the water. Stir over a low heat until dissolved. Boil until the syrup reaches a temperature of 120°C/ 250°F on a sugar thermometer. Remove from the heat.

5 Whisk the egg white until stiff. Add the syrup in a thin stream, whisking all the time. Continue to whisk until the mixture is very thick and fluffy.

6 Place the cake on a board. Spread the icing over the top and sides of the cake, gently teasing it down the sides to coat the cake evenly. Sprinkle the orange rind over the top of the cake. Slide a knife around the edge under the cake, then transfer it to a platter to serve.

NUTRITIONAL INFORMATION: Energy 149.5kcal/637.3kJ; Protein 2.4g; Carbohydrate 36.4g, of which sugars 33g; Fat 0.4g, of which saturates 0.2g; Cholesterol 0mg; Calcium 23.3mg; Fibre 0.3g; Sodium 53.5mg.

Black Forest Gateau

This luscious light chocolate sponge, moist with Kirsch, cherries and cream, is eternally popular.

ingredients

SERVES EIGHT TO TEN

- 5 eggs
- 200g/7oz/scant 1 cup caster (superfine) sugar
- 5ml/1 tsp vanilla extract
- 50g/2oz/½ cup plain (all-purpose) flour
- 50g/2oz/½ cup unsweetened cocoa powder
- 115g/4oz/½ cup unsalted (sweet) butter, melted

For the filling and topping

- 60ml/4 tbsp Kirsch
- 600ml/1 pint/2½ cups double (heavy) cream
- 30ml/2 tbsp icing (confectioners') sugar
- 2.5ml/½ tsp vanilla extract
- 675g/1½lb jar stoned (pitted) morello cherries, drained

To decorate

- chocolate, grated and in curls
- fresh or drained canned morello cherries

1 Preheat the oven to 180°C/350°F/Gas 4. Grease three 19cm/7½in sandwich cake tins (pans) and line the base with baking parchment.

2 Whisk the eggs with the sugar and vanilla in a large bowl until pale and very thick. Sift the flour and cocoa powder over the mixture and fold in. Stir in the melted butter.

3 Divide the mixture equally among the three tins, smoothing with a palette knife or metal spatula.

4 Bake for 15 minutes, until risen and springy to the touch. Cool in the tins for 5 minutes, then turn out on to wire racks and leave to cool completely.

5 Prick each layer with a skewer, then sprinkle with Kirsch. Whip the cream until it starts to thicken, then beat in the icing sugar and vanilla until the mixture begins to hold its shape.

6 Spread a cake layer with a layer of the cream and top with a quarter of the cherries.

7 Spread a second cake with cream and cherries, then place on top of the first. Top with the final layer. Spread the remaining cream all over the cake. Press grated chocolate over the sides and decorate the top with the chocolate curls and cherries to finish.

NUTRITIONAL INFORMATION: Energy 570kcal/2371kJ; Protein 2.9g; Carbohydrate 44g, of which sugars 39.6g; Fat 42.8g, of which saturates 25.7g; Cholesterol 107mg; Calcium 67mg; Fibre 1.2g; Sodium 137mg.

Chocolate Raisin Cheesecake

This crisp chocolate shortbread has a creamy chocolate-chip filling and a sticky chocolate glaze.

ingredients

SERVES EIGHT TO TEN

- 75g/3oz/¾ cup plain (all-purpose) flour
- 45ml/3 tbsp unsweetened cocoa powder
- 75g/3oz/½ cup semolina
- 50g/2oz/¼ cup caster sugar
- 115g/4oz/½ cup unsalted (sweet) butter, softened

For the filling

- 225g/8oz/¯ cup cream cheese
- 120ml/4fl oz/½ cup natural (plain) yogurt
- 2 eggs, beaten
- 75g/3oz/6 tbsp caster (superfine) sugar
- finely grated rind of 1 lemon
- 75g/3oz/½ cup raisins
- 45ml/3 tbsp plain (semisweet) chocolate chips

For the topping

- 75g/3oz plain (semisweet) chocolate, broken into squares
- 30ml/2 tbsp golden (light corn) syrup
- 40g/1½oz/3 tbsp butter

1 Preheat the oven to 150°C/ 300°F/Gas 2. Sift the flour and cocoa powder into a mixing bowl and stir in the semolina and sugar. Using your fingertips, work the butter into the flour mixture until it makes a firm dough.

2 Press the dough evenly into the base of a 22cm/8½in springform tin (pan). Prick the dough all over with a fork and bake in the oven for 15 minutes, until lightly cooked and beginning to firm up but not browned.

3 Meanwhile, make the filling. In a large bowl, beat the cream cheese with the yogurt, eggs and sugar until evenly mixed. Stir in the lemon rind, raisins and chocolate chips.

4 Smooth the cream cheese mixture over the chocolate shortbread base and bake the cheesecake for a further 35–45 minutes, or until the filling is pale gold on top and just set. Leave the cheesecake to cool in the tin and then chill it for a few hours, if possible, before making the topping.

5 For the topping, melt the chocolate, syrup and butter in a heatproof bowl over a pan of simmering water, stirring often. Pour over the cheesecake and leave to set.

NUTRITIONAL INFORMATION: Energy 441kcal/1841kJ; Protein 5.8g; Carbohydrate 41.4g, of which sugars 29.3g; Fat 29.3g, of which saturates 17.7g Cholesterol 93mg; Calcium 86mg; Fibre 1.4g; Sodium 243mg.

Chocolate Redcurrant Torte

This torte makes the perfect accompaniment to strong coffee for an afternoon break.

ingredients

SERVES EIGHT TO TEN

- 115g/4oz/½ cup unsalted (sweet) butter, softened
- 115g/4oz/⅔ cup dark muscovado (molasses) sugar
- 2 eggs
- 150ml/¼ pint/⅔ cup sour cream
- 150g/5oz/1¼ cups self-raising (self-rising) flour, plus a small amount for dusting
- 5ml/1 tsp baking powder
- 45ml/3 tbsp unsweetened cocoa powder
- 75g/3oz/¾ cup stemmed redcurrants, plus 115g/4oz/1 cup redcurrant sprigs, to decorate

For the icing

- 150g/5oz plain (semisweet) chocolate, broken into squares
- 45ml/3 tbsp redcurrant jelly
- 30ml/2 tbsp dark rum
- 120ml/4fl oz/½ cup double (heavy) cream

1 Preheat the oven to 180°C/350°F/Gas 4. Grease a 1.2 litre/2 pint/5 cup ring tin (pan) and dust it lightly with flour, tilting and tapping the tin.

2 Cream the butter with the sugar in a mixing bowl until pale and fluffy. Beat in the eggs and sour cream until thoroughly mixed.

3 Sift the flour, baking powder and cocoa over the mixture, then gently fold in lightly and evenly. Fold in the stemmed redcurrants.

4 Spoon the mixture into the prepared tin and smooth the surface level. Bake the cake for about 40–50 minutes, or until well risen and firm. Turn out on to a wire rack and leave to cool completely.

5 Make the icing. Mix the chocolate, redcurrant jelly and rum in a heatproof bowl. Set the bowl over a pan of simmering water and heat gently, stirring occasionally, until the chocolate and jelly have melted. Remove from the heat and stir in the cream.

6 Transfer the cooked cake to a serving plate. Spoon the icing slowly and evenly over the cake, allowing it to drizzle down the sides. Leave to set in a cool place but do not chill. Decorate with redcurrant sprigs just before serving.

NUTRITIONAL INFORMATION: Energy 347kcal/1444kJ; Protein 3.7g; Carbohydrate 26.5g, of which sugars 25.9g; Fat 25.2g, of which saturates 15.3g; Cholesterol 89mg; Calcium 50mg; Fibre 1.2g; Sodium 138mg.

Chocolate Beetroot Cake

Beetroot and chocolate are surprisingly good together, especially with a rich ganache frosting.

ingredients

SERVES TEN TO TWELVE

- unsweetened cocoa powder, for dusting
- 225g/8oz can cooked whole beetroot (beet), drained and juice reserved, grated
- 115g/4oz/½ cup unsalted (sweet) butter, softened
- 425g/15oz/2½ cups soft light brown sugar
- 3 eggs
- 15ml/1 tbsp vanilla extract
- 75g/3oz dark (bittersweet) chocolate, melted
- 225g/8oz/2 cups plain (all-purpose) flour
- 10ml/2 tsp baking powder
- 120ml/4fl oz/½ cup buttermilk
- chocolate curls or coarsely grated chocolate, to decorate

For the ganache frosting

- 475ml/16fl oz/2 cups whipping cream or double (heavy) cream
- 500g/1¼lb fine quality (dark) bittersweet or plain chocolate, chopped into small pieces
- 15ml/1 tbsp vanilla extract

1 Preheat the oven to 180°C/350°F/Gas 4. Grease two 23cm/9in cake tins (pans) and dust with cocoa powder. Mix the beetroot with the juice. Beat the butter, sugar, eggs and vanilla extract until pale. Beat in the melted chocolate. Sift the flour with the baking powder.

2 Gradually beat in the flour and baking powder, alternately with the buttermilk. Add the beetroot and juice and beat for 1 minute. Divide between the tins and bake for 30 minutes, until risen, firm and springy.

3 Cool the cakes for 10 minutes, then turn them out on a wire rack and cool completely.

4 For the frosting, heat the cream in a pan over a medium heat until it just boils, stirring often. Remove from the heat. Stir in the chocolate and vanilla until melted and smooth. Cool and chill. Stir every 10 minutes for 1 hour, until spreadable.

5 Sandwich the cake together using one-third of the frosting. Spread the remaining frosting all over the cake, top and sides.

6 Decorate with chocolate curls or coarsely grated chocolate. Leave to set for 20–30 minutes. Chill for 2–4 hours before serving.

NUTRITIONAL INFORMATION: Energy 699kcal/2925kJ; Protein 7.4g; Carbohydrate 85.1g, of which sugars 70.3g; Fat 38.9g, of which saturates 23.5g; Cholesterol 113mg; Calcium 109mg; Fibre 2.1g; Sodium 108mg.

Chocolate Potato Cake

The surprising addition of mashed potato makes this cake moist and delicious.

ingredients

MAKES A 23cm/9in CAKE

- 200g/7oz/1 cup sugar
- 250g/9oz/generous 1 cup butter
- 4 eggs, separated
- 275g/10oz dark (bittersweet) chocolate
- 75g/3oz/¾ cup mashed potato
- 225g/8oz/2 cups self-raising (self-rising) flour
- 5ml/1 tsp cinnamon
- 45ml/3 tbsp milk

To garnish

- white and dark (bittersweet) chocolate shavings

1 Preheat the oven to 180°C/350°F/Gas 4. Grease and line a 23cm/9in round cake tin with baking parchment. Cream together the sugar and 225g/8oz/1 cup of the butter until light, then beat the egg yolks into the mixture one at a time until it is smooth and creamy.

2 Finely chop or grate 175g/6oz of the chocolate and stir it into the mixture. Pass the mashed potato through a sieve (strainer) and stir it into the chocolate mixture.

3 Sift together the flour and cinnamon and fold into the creamed mixture with the milk. Whisk the egg whites until they hold stiff but not dry peaks, and fold into the cake mixture.

4 Spoon into the prepared tin. Smooth the top, making a slight hollow in the middle to help keep the surface level during cooking. Bake for 1¼ hours, until a skewer inserted into the centre comes out clean. Cool the cake slightly in the tin, then turn out to cool on a wire rack.

5 Meanwhile, make the chocolate icing. Break up the remaining chocolate and place in a heatproof bowl. Stand the bowl over a pan of barely simmering water. Add the remaining butter and stir well until the chocolate has melted.

6 Peel off the lining paper and trim the top of the cake so that it is level. Pour the chocolate icing on top of the cake and smooth it evenly with a palette knife or metal spatula. Allow to set. Decorate with dark and white chocolate shavings.

NUTRITIONAL INFORMATION: Energy 5749kcal/24034kJ; Protein 87.1g; Carbohydrate 590.9g, of which sugars 391.8g; Fat 354.8g, of which saturates 188.1g; Cholesterol 1465mg; Calcium 1408mg; Fibre 21.5g; Sodium 2731mg.

Mocha Chocolate Sponge

Mocha may refer to the variety of coffee or, as here, to a combination of coffee and chocolate.

ingredients

SERVES TEN

- 25ml/1½ tbsp strong-flavoured ground coffee
- 175ml/6fl oz/¾ cup milk
- 115g/4oz/8 tbsp butter
- 115g/4oz/½ cup soft light brown sugar
- 1 egg, lightly beaten
- 185g/6½oz/1⅔ cups self-raising (self-rising) flour
- 5ml/1 tsp bicarbonate of soda (baking soda)
- 60ml/4 tbsp creamy liqueur, such as Baileys or Irish Velvet

For the chocolate icing

- 200g/7oz plain (semisweet) chocolate, broken into pieces
- 75g/3oz/6 tbsp unsalted (sweet) butter, cubed
- 120ml/4fl oz/½ cup double (heavy) cream

1 Preheat the oven to 180°C/350°F/Gas 4. Grease and line a 18cm/7in round fixed-base cake tin (pan) with baking parchment.

2 To make the cake, put the coffee in a jug (pitcher). Heat the milk to near-boiling and pour it over the coffee. Leave to infuse for 4 minutes, then strain through a sieve (strainer) and allow to cool.

3 Gently melt the butter and sugar. Pour into a bowl and cool for 2 minutes, then stir in the egg.

4 Sift the flour over the mixture and fold in. Blend the bicarbonate of soda with the coffee-flavoured milk and gradually stir into the mixture.

5 Pour the cake mixture into the tin and smooth the surface. Bake the cake for 40 minutes, until well-risen and firm. Cool in the tin for about 10 minutes.

6 Gradually spoon the liqueur over the cake and leave until cold. Loosen the edges with a palette knife and turn out on to a wire rack.

7 To make the icing, place the broken chocolate in a heatproof bowl over a pan of barely simmering water and stir until melted. Remove from the heat and stir in the butter and cream until smooth. Allow to cool.

8 Spread the icing over the top and sides of the cake using a palette knife or metal spatula. Leave to set before serving.

NUTRITIONAL INFORMATION: Energy 444kcal/1853kJ; Protein 4.2g; Carbohydrate 41.2g, of which sugars 27.3g; Fat 29.7g, of which saturates 17.6g; Cholesterol 78mg; Calcium 112mg; Fibre 1.1g; Sodium 206mg.

Hazelnut Chocolate Cake

This silky chocolate cake marries the satisfying crunch of hazelnuts with just a hint of orange.

ingredients

SERVES TEN

- 150g/5oz plain (semisweet) chocolate
- 115g/4oz/½ cup unsalted (sweet) butter, softened
- 115g/4oz/½ cup caster (superfine) sugar
- 4 eggs, separated
- 115g/4oz/1 cup ground lightly toasted hazelnuts
- 50g/2oz/1 cup fresh white breadcrumbs
- grated rind of 1½ oranges
- 30ml/2 tbsp strained marmalade, warmed
- 60ml/4 tbsp chopped hazelnuts, to decorate

For the icing

- 150g/5oz plain (semisweet) chocolate, chopped
- 50g/2oz/¼ cup unsalted (sweet) butter, diced

1 Preheat the oven to 180°C/ 350°F/Gas 4. Line and butter a 23cm/9in round cake tin (pan).

2 Melt the chocolate in a heatproof bowl set over a pan of simmering water and set aside.

3 Beat the butter and sugar together, then gradually add the egg yolks, beating well. The mixture may curdle slightly. Beat in the chocolate, then the hazelnuts, breadcrumbs and orange rind.

4 Whisk the egg whites until stiff, then fold them into the mixture. Transfer the mixture to the tin. Bake for 40–45 minutes, until risen, set and springy to the touch. Remove from the oven, cover with a damp dish towel for 5 minutes, then transfer to a wire rack to cool.

5 For the icing, place the chocolate and butter in a heatproof bowl over a pan of simmering water and stir until melted. Leave to cool slightly.

6 Spread the marmalade over the cake. Spoon on the icing and spread evenly over the top. Scatter the nuts over the icing while it is soft, then leave to set.

NUTRITIONAL INFORMATION: Energy 490kcal/2040kJ; Protein 7.2g; Carbohydrate 38.2g, of which sugars 33.8g; Fat 35.4g, of which saturates 15.1g Cholesterol 113mg; Calcium 62mg; Fibre 2g; Sodium 172mg.

Chocolate Fudge Cake

With chocolate fudge frosting, this cake couldn't be easier to make or more wonderful to eat!

ingredients

SERVES SIX TO EIGHT

- 115g/4oz plain (semisweet) chocolate, broken into squares
- 175g/6oz/¾ cup unsalted (sweet) butter or margarine, softened
- 200g/7oz/generous 1 cup light muscovado (brown) sugar
- 5ml/1 tsp vanilla extract
- 3 eggs, beaten
- 150ml/¼ pint/⅔ cup Greek (US strained plain) yogurt
- 150g/5oz/1¼ cups self-raising (self-rising) flour
- icing (confectioners') sugar and chocolate curls, to decorate

For the frosting

- 115g/4oz plain dark chocolate, broken into squares
- 50g/2oz/4 tbsp unsalted (sweet) butter
- 350g/12oz/3 cups icing (confectioners') sugar
- 90ml/6 tbsp Greek (US strained plain) yogurt

1 Preheat the oven to 190°C/375°F/Gas 5. Grease two 20cm/8in round sandwich cake tins (pans) and line the bases with baking parchment.

2 Melt the chocolate gently in a heatproof bowl set over a pan of simmering water.

3 In a large bowl, cream the butter or margarine with the sugar until light and fluffy. Beat in the vanilla extract, then gradually add the beaten eggs, beating well after each addition.

4 Stir in the melted chocolate and yogurt evenly. Fold in the flour with a metal spoon.

5 Divide the mixture between the tins. Bake for 25–30 minutes, or until the cakes are firm to the touch. Turn out and cool on a wire rack.

6 For the frosting, melt the chocolate and butter in a pan over a low heat. Remove from the heat and stir in the icing sugar and yogurt. Mix until smooth, then beat until cooling and thickening slightly.

7 Use a third of the mixture to sandwich the cakes together. Spread the rest over the top and sides of the cake. Sprinkle with icing sugar and chocolate curls. Leave to set.

NUTRITIONAL INFORMATION: Energy 753kcal/3160kJ; Protein 8g; Carbohydrate 105.4g, of which sugars 90.9g; Fat 36.6g, of which saturates 21.7g; Cholesterol 133mg; Calcium 133mg; Fibre 1.3g; Sodium 224mg.

Rich Chocolate Leaf Gateau

Thick, creamy chocolate ganache and chocolate leaves decorate this mouth-watering gateau.

ingredients

SERVES TWELVE TO FOURTEEN

- 150ml/¼ pint/⅔ cup milk
- 75g/3oz dark (bittersweet) chocolate, broken into squares
- 175g/6oz/¾ cup unsalted (sweet) butter, softened
- 250g/9oz/1½ cups light muscovado (brown) sugar
- 3 eggs
- 250g/9oz/2¼ cups plain (all-purpose) flour
- 10ml/2 tsp baking powder
- 75ml/5 tbsp single (light) cream

For the filling and topping

- 60ml/4 tbsp raspberry conserve
- 1 quantity chocolate ganache frosting (see p25 for recipe)
- dark (bittersweet) and white chocolate leaves

1 Preheat the oven to 190°C/375°F/Gas 5. Grease two 22cm/8½ in sandwich cake tins (pans) and line the base of each with baking parchment.

2 In a pan, stir the milk and chocolate over a low heat until the chocolate has melted. Remove from the heat and allow to cool slightly.

3 Cream the butter with the sugar in a bowl until pale and fluffy. Beat in the eggs one at a time, beating well after each addition.

4 Sift the flour and baking powder over the mixture and fold in using a large metal spoon. Stir in the melted chocolate mixture with the cream, mixing until smooth.

5 Divide the mixture between the prepared tins and level the tops. Bake for 30–35 minutes, or until the cakes are well risen, firm and springy to the touch. Allow the cakes to cool in the tins for a few minutes, then carefully turn them out on to wire racks and leave to cool completely before filling.

6 Sandwich the two cake layers together with the raspberry conserve.

7 Prepare the chocolate ganache and spread it over the top and sides of the cake. Swirl the ganache with a knife.

8 Place the cake on a serving plate, then decorate the top with the dark and white chocolate leaves.

NUTRITIONAL INFORMATION: Energy 476kcal/1986kJ; Protein 5.3g; Carbohydrate 49.4g, of which sugars 35.7g; Fat 29.9g, of which saturates 18.2g; Cholesterol 102mg; Calcium 84mg; Fibre 1g; Sodium 108mg.

Chocolate Chestnut Cake

This combination is an international favourite – a chocolate cake with chestnut cream filling.

ingredients

SERVES EIGHT TO TWELVE

- 225g/8oz/1 cup butter, at room temperature
- 225g/8oz/generous 1 cup caster (superfine) sugar
- 200g/7oz plain (semisweet) chocolate, melted
- 6 eggs, separated
- 130g/4½oz/generous 1 cup plain (all-purpose) flour, sifted
- chocolate curls, to decorate

For the filling

- 250ml/8fl oz/1 cup double (heavy) cream, lightly whipped
- 450g/1lb/1¾ cups canned chestnut purée
- 115g/4oz/generous ½ cup caster (superfine) sugar

For the topping

- 150g/5oz/10 tbsp unsalted (sweet) butter
- 150g/5oz/1¼ cups icing (confectioners') sugar, sifted
- 115g/4oz plain (semisweet) chocolate, melted

1 Preheat the oven to 180°C/350°F/Gas 4. Grease and line the base and sides of a 20–23cm/8–9in round cake tin (pan). Cream the butter and sugar together in a bowl until pale and fluffy. Stir in the melted chocolate and egg yolks. Fold the flour carefully into the chocolate mixture.

2 Whisk the egg whites until stiff. Add a spoonful of the egg white to the chocolate mixture to loosen it, then carefully fold in the remainder. Spoon the mixture into the tin.

3 Bake the cake for 45–50 minutes, or until firm to the touch and a skewer inserted into the middle comes out clean. Cool on a wire rack. When cold, peel off the lining paper and slice the cake into two layers.

4 Mix the filling ingredients together in a bowl. Sandwich the two cake halves together firmly with the chestnut filling.

5 Cream together the butter and sugar for the topping before stirring in the melted chocolate.

6 Using a dampened knife, carefully spread the chocolate topping over the sides and top of the cake. Chill for up to 60 minutes before serving if possible, and then decorate the cake with chocolate curls.

NUTRITIONAL INFORMATION: Energy 731kcal/3055kJ; Protein 3.8g; Carbohydrate 82g, of which sugars 62.4g; Fat 45.4g, of which saturates 27.9g; Cholesterol 97mg; Calcium 79mg; Fibre 2.5g; Sodium 202mg.

Chocolate Chip Walnut Loaf

This sweet and nutty loaf cake includes a hint of juicy currants.

ingredients

MAKES ONE LOAF

- 115g/4oz/½ cup caster (superfine) sugar
- 115g/4oz/1 cup plain (all-purpose) flour
- 5ml/1 tsp baking powder
- 30ml/4 tbsp cornflour (cornstarch)
- 115g/4oz/½ cup butter, softened
- 2 eggs, beaten
- 5ml/1 tsp vanilla extract
- 30ml/2 tbsp currants or raisins
- 25g/1oz/¼ cup walnuts, finely chopped
- grated rind of ½ lemon
- 45ml/3 tbsp plain (semisweet) chocolate chips
- icing (confectioners') sugar, for dusting

1 Preheat the oven to 180°C/350°F/Gas 4. Grease and line a 22 x 12cm/8½ x 4½in loaf tin (pan).

2 Sprinkle 25ml/1½ tbsp of the caster sugar into the pan and tilt to distribute the sugar in an even layer over the bottom and sides. Shake out any excess sugar and discard.

3 Gently sift the flour, baking powder and cornflour into a large mixing bowl. Repeat twice more. Set aside.

4 Using an electric mixer, cream the butter in a bowl until very soft.

5 Add the remaining sugar and the butter and continue beating until light and fluffy. Then add the eggs, one at a time, beating well after each addition.

6 Fold the sifted dry ingredients into the butter mixture, in three batches. Take care not to overmix the ingredients as this will knock out the air.

7 Fold in the vanilla extract, currants or raisins, walnuts, lemon rind and chocolate chips, until just blended.

8 Pour the mixture into the prepared tin and bake for 45–50 minutes. Cool in the loaf tin for 5 minutes before transferring to a rack to cool completely.

9 Place the cake on a plate and dust with icing sugar.

NUTRITIONAL INFORMATION: Energy 3759kcal/15650kJ; Protein 60.1g; Carbohydrate 294g, of which sugars 149.5g; Fat 268.6g, of which saturates 76.5g; Cholesterol 626mg; Calcium 543mg; Fibre 12.5g; Sodium 913mg.

Chocolate Marzipan Loaf

Inside this ordinary-looking loaf there are creamy chunks of marzipan and chips of chocolate.

ingredients

MAKES ONE LOAF

- 130g/3½oz marzipan
- 60ml/4 tbsp plain (semisweet) chocolate chips
- 115g/4oz/½ cup unsalted (sweet) butter, softened
- 150g/5oz/scant 1 cup light muscovado (brown) sugar
- 2 eggs, beaten
- 45ml/3 tbsp unsweetened cocoa powder
- 150g/5oz/1¼ cups self-raising (self-rising) flour

cook's tip

Marzipan keeps well in the freezer, so if you have any leftover, wrap it in clear film (plastic wrap) and place in a freezer bag. The paste does not freeze rock-hard and it can be cut into chunks with a heavy knife while frozen.

1 Preheat the oven to 180°C/350°F/Gas 4. Grease a 900g/2lb loaf tin (pan) and line the base with baking parchment.

2 Chop the marzipan, turn into a bowl and mix with the chocolate chips.

3 Cream the butter and sugar together in a large bowl until light and fluffy.

4 Gradually add the beaten eggs, beating well after each addition to combine.

5 Gently sift the cocoa powder and flour over the mixture and fold in evenly and lightly with a metal spoon.

6 Set aside about 60ml/4 tbsp of the marzipan mixture and fold the rest evenly into the cake mixture.

7 Scrape the mixture into the prepared tin, level and scatter with the reserved marzipan and chocolate chips.

8 Bake for 45 minutes, or until the loaf is risen and firm. Cool for a few minutes in the tin, then turn out on to a wire rack to cool completely.

NUTRITIONAL INFORMATION: Energy 2919kcal/12240kJ; Protein 46.1g; Carbohydrate 368.6g, of which sugars 248.6g; Fat 150.7g, of which saturates 80.5g; Cholesterol 629mg; Calcium 513mg; Fibre 14.1g; Sodium 1305mg.

Chocolate Marmalade Cake

Don't be alarmed at the amount of cream in this recipe – it's deliciously naughty but necessary.

ingredients

SERVES EIGHT

- 115g/4oz plain (semisweet) chocolate, broken into squares
- 3 eggs
- 200g/7oz/scant 1 cup caster (superfine) sugar
- 175ml/6fl oz/¾ cup sour cream
- 200g/7oz/1¾ cups self-raising (self-rising) flour

For the filling and glaze

- 175g/6oz/⅔ cup bitter orange marmalade
- 115g/4oz plain (semisweet) chocolate, broken into squares
- 60ml/4 tbsp sour cream
- shredded orange rind, to decorate

1 Preheat the oven to 180°C/350°F/Gas 4. Grease a 900g/2lb loaf tin (pan), then line it with baking parchment.

2 Melt the chocolate in a heatproof bowl over a pan of simmering water, stirring often until smooth.

3 Combine the eggs and sugar in a large bowl. Whisk the mixture until it is thick and creamy, then stir in the sour cream and chocolate. Then carefully fold in the flour.

4 Spoon the mixture into the tin and bake for 1 hour, until well risen and firm to the touch. Cool for a few minutes, then turn out on to a wire rack and cool completely.

5 For the filling, spoon two-thirds of the marmalade into a pan and melt, stirring occasionally, over a low heat.

6 Melt the chocolate in a heatproof bowl over a pan of simmering water and stir it into the marmalade with the sour cream.

7 Slice the cake across into three layers and sandwich together with half the filling. Spread the rest over the top of the cake and leave to set. Spoon the remaining filling over the cake and scatter with orange rind.

NUTRITIONAL INFORMATION: Energy 475kcal/2004kJ; Protein 7.1g; Carbohydrate 80.1g, of which sugars 60.8g; Fat 16.3g, of which saturates 9.1g; Cholesterol 91mg; Calcium 101mg; Fibre 1.6g; Sodium 56mg.

Madeleines

These little tea cakes, baked in a shell-shaped cups, are best eaten on the day they are made.

ingredients

MAKES TWELVE

- 165g/5½oz/generous 1¼ cups plain (all-purpose) flour
- 5ml/1 tsp baking powder
- 2 eggs
- 75g/3oz/¾ cup icing (confectioners') sugar, plus extra for dusting
- grated rind of 1 lemon or orange
- 15ml/1 tbsp lemon or orange juice
- 75g/3oz/6 tbsp unsalted (sweet) butter, melted and slightly cooled

cook's tips

- *These cakes look sweet baked in the traditional Madeleine tins (pans), as pictured, but all kinds of novelty cake tins, such as flowers, stars and hearts are available.*

- *Drizzle orange-flavoured glacé icing over the tops, and for special occasions mix the icing with a little rum.*

1 Preheat the oven to 190°C/375°F/Gas 5. Grease a 12-cup madeleine tin (pan), taking care to grease each of the flutes thoroughly or the cakes will stick. Sift together the flour and the baking powder.

2 Beat the eggs and icing sugar in a large bowl until thick and creamy. Gently fold in the lemon or orange rind and juice.

3 Beginning with the flour mixture, alternately fold in the flour and melted butter in four batches.

4 Leave to stand for 10 minutes, then spoon into the tin. Tap gently to release any air.

5 Bake for 15 minutes, rotating halfway through cooking. The madeleines should be risen, firm and evenly golden in colour.

6 Turn the cakes on to a wire rack to cool completely and dust them lightly with icing sugar before serving.

NUTRITIONAL INFORMATION: Energy 130kcal/547kJ; Protein 2.4g; Carbohydrate 17.3g, of which sugars 6.8g; Fat 6.2g, of which saturates 3.5g; Cholesterol 45mg; Calcium 28mg; Fibre 0.4g; Sodium 50mg.

Coconut Cakes

These moist coconut cakes are commonplace in Sweden. They are best served straight from the oven.

ingredients

MAKES FIFTEEN TO TWENTY

- 1 vanilla pod (bean)
- 120ml/4fl oz/½ cup double (heavy) cream
- 200g/7oz desiccated (dry unsweetened shredded) coconut
- 200g/4oz/1 cup caster (superfine) sugar
- 1 egg

variation

Shape the coconut mixture into hollow nests before baking. Serve filled with ice cream and fresh fruit for a dessert that children will love.

2 Preheat the oven to 200°C/400°F/Gas 6. Line a baking sheet with baking parchment. Remove the vanilla pod from the cream and pour the cream into a bowl. Add the coconut, sugar and egg and mix together.

1 Split open the vanilla pod and put in a pan with the cream. Heat gently until bubbles start to form round the edge of the cream in the pan, then remove from the heat and leave the cream to infuse for 20 minutes.

cook's tip

Don't discard the vanilla pod after you have used it to make the vanilla cream. Rinse it well, leave to dry and then keep it in a jar to use again.

3 Spoon the mixture in piles on to the prepared baking sheet. Bake in the oven for 12–15 minutes, until golden brown and slightly crisp on top. Leave the cakes to cool slightly before transferring them to a cooling rack.

NUTRITIONAL INFORMATION: Energy 177kcal/740kJ; Protein 1.4g; Carbohydrate 14.9g, of which sugars 14.9g; Fat 13g, of which saturates 9.9g; Cholesterol 23.6mg; Calcium 16mg; Fibre 1.8g; Sodium 10.9mg.

Honey and Spice Cakes

These cakes are fragrant with honey and cinnamon. They tend to rise higher when baked in paper cases.

ingredients

MAKES EIGHTEEN

- 250g/9oz/2 cups plain (all-purpose) flour
- 5ml/1 tsp ground cinnamon
- 5ml/1 tsp bicarbonate of soda (baking soda)
- 125g/4½oz/½ cup butter, softened
- 125g/4½oz/10 tbsp soft light brown sugar
- 1 large (US extra large) egg, separated
- 125g/4½oz clear honey
- about 60ml/4 tbsp milk
- caster (superfine) sugar for sprinkling

variation

Use 2.5 ml/½ tsp ground cardamom seeds instead of the cinnamon and brown sugar. Add 125g/4½oz chopped pistachio nuts with the flour.

1 Preheat the oven to 200°C/400°F/Gas 6. Grease an 18-cup bun tin (pan) or, alternatively, line with paper cases.

2 Sift the flour into a large mixing bowl with the cinnamon and bicarbonate of soda.

3 Beat the butter with the sugar until light and fluffy. Beat in the egg yolk, then gradually add the honey.

4 With a large metal spoon and using a cutting action, fold in the flour mixture, adding sufficient milk to make a soft mixture that will just drop off the spoon.

5 In a separate bowl, whisk the egg white until stiff peaks form. Using a large metal spoon, fold the egg white into the cake mixture. Do not overmix.

6 Divide the mixture among the paper cases or the holes in the prepared tin. Put into the hot oven and cook for 15–20 minutes, or until risen, firm to the touch and golden brown.

7 Sprinkle the tops lightly with caster sugar and leave to cool completely on a wire rack.

NUTRITIONAL INFORMATION: Energy 152kcal/639kJ; Protein 1.9g; Carbohydrate 23.6g, of which sugars 13g; Fat 6.3g, of which saturates 3.8g Cholesterol 26mg; Calcium 30mg; Fibre 0.4g; Sodium 49mg.

Iced Fancies

These cakes are ideal for a children's tea-party. Ready-made decorations may be used for speed.

ingredients

MAKES SIXTEEN

- 115g/4oz/½ cup butter, at room temperature
- 225g/8oz/generous 1 cup caster (superfine) sugar
- 2 eggs, at room temperature
- 175g/6oz/1½ cups plain (all-purpose) flour
- 1.5ml/¼ tsp salt
- 7.5ml/1½ tsp baking powder
- 120ml/4fl oz/½ cup milk
- 5ml/1 tsp vanilla extract

For the icing

- 2 large egg whites
- 400g/14oz/3½ cups sifted icing (confectioners') sugar
- 1–2 drops glycerine
- juice of 1 lemon
- food colourings of your choice
- coloured vermicelli, and crystallized lemon and orange slices, to decorate

1 Preheat the oven to 190°C/375°F/Gas 5. Line a 16-cup bun tin (pan) with paper cases.

2 Cream the butter and sugar until light and fluffy. Add the eggs, one at a time, beating well after each addition.

3 Sift over and stir in the flour, salt and baking powder, alternating with the milk. Add the vanilla extract.

4 Half-fill the cups and bake for 20 minutes, or until risen and springy

5 Leave the cakes to cool in the tray for 5 minutes, then transfer to a wire rack and leave to cool completely before decorating. The baked cakes can be frozen at this stage, ready for decorating later.

6 To make the icing, beat the egg whites until stiff. Gradually add the sugar, glycerine and lemon juice, and beat for about 1 minute.

7 Tint the icing with the different food colourings, and use to ice the tops of the cakes.

8 When the icing has set, decorate with coloured vermicelli and crystallized lemon and orange slices, or make freehand decorations using a paper piping (icing) bag.

9 Arrange the cakes on a plate. Cover with clear film (plastic wrap) until ready to serve.

NUTRITIONAL INFORMATION: Energy 259kcal/1094kJ; Protein 2.7g; Carbohydrate 49.7g, of which sugars 41.4g; Fat 6.9g, of which saturates 4g; Cholesterol 40mg; Calcium 50mg; Fibre 0.3g; Sodium 66mg

Vanilla Chocolate Fairy Cakes

These temptingly sweet fairy cakes have a rich, vanilla-flavoured topping.

ingredients

MAKES TWENTY-FOUR

- 115g/4oz plain (semisweet) chocolate, chopped into pieces
- 15ml/1 tbsp water
- 275g/10oz/2½ cups plain (all-purpose) flour
- 5ml/1 tsp baking powder
- 2.5ml/½ tsp bicarbonate of soda (baking soda)
- pinch of salt
- 300g/11oz/scant 1½ cups caster (superfine) sugar
- 175g/6oz/¾ cup butter or margarine, at room temperature
- 150ml/¼ pint/⅔ cup milk
- 5ml/1 tsp vanilla extract
- 3 eggs

For the icing

- 40g/1½ oz/3 tbsp butter or margarine
- 115g/4oz/1 cup icing (confectioners') sugar
- 2.5ml/½ tsp vanilla extract
- 15–30ml/1–2 tbsp milk

1 Preheat the oven to 180°C/350°F/Gas 4. Grease a 24-cup bun tin (pan) or, alternatively, line with paper cases.

2 For the icing, soften the butter. Place it in a bowl and stir in the icing sugar, a little at a time, and vanilla extract. A drop at a time, beat in enough milk to make a creamy mixture. Cover and set aside.

3 Melt the chocolate with the water in a heatproof bowl over simmering water. Remove from the heat.

4 Sift the flour, baking powder, bicarbonate of soda, salt and sugar into a large bowl. Then add the chocolate mixture, butter or margarine, milk and vanilla extract.

5 With a hand-held electric mixer on medium speed, beat the mixture until smooth. Increase the speed to high and beat for 2 minutes.

6 Add the eggs, one at a time, and beat for 1 minute after each addition. Divide among the tins.

7 Bake for 20–25 minutes, until the cakes are risen and springy. Cool in the tins for 10 minutes, then turn out to cool completely on a wire rack. Spread the top of each cake with the icing, swirling it into a peak in the centre.

NUTRITIONAL INFORMATION: Energy 228kcal/957kJ; Protein 2.5g; Carbohydrate 30.6g, of which sugars 21g; Fat 11.5g, of which saturates 3.3g; Cholesterol 33mg; Calcium 40mg; Fibre 0.5g; Sodium 95mg.

Minty Chocolate Cupcakes

The delicious chocolate mint glaze gives these a welcome twist on the classic chocolate cupcake.

ingredients

MAKES TWELVE

- 225g/8oz/2 cups plain (all-purpose) flour
- 5ml/1 tsp bicarbonate of soda (baking soda)
- 50g/2oz/½ cup unsweetened cocoa powder
- 150g/5oz/10 tbsp unsalted (sweet) butter, softened
- 350g/12oz/1½ cups caster (superfine) sugar
- 3 eggs
- 5ml/1 tsp peppermint extract
- 250ml/8 fl oz/1 cup milk

For the mint cream filling

- 300ml/½ pint/1¼ cups double (heavy) cream or whipping cream
- 5ml/1 tsp peppermint extract

For the chocolate mint glaze

- 175g/6oz plain (semisweet) chocolate, chopped into small pieces
- 115g/4oz/½ cup unsalted (sweet) butter
- 5ml/1 tsp peppermint extract

1 Preheat oven to 180°C/350°F/Gas 4. Line a 12-cup bun tin (pan) with paper cases, using the cases double if they are thin. Sift the flour, bicarbonate of soda and cocoa powder into a bowl.

2 In a large bowl, beat the butter and sugar with a hand-held electric mixer for about 3–5 minutes, until light and creamy. Add the eggs, one at a time, beating after each addition and adding a small amount of the flour. Beat in the peppermint extract.

3 Gently beat in the flour and cocoa mixture alternately with the milk, until just blended. Spoon into the paper cases. Bake for 15 minutes, until risen and springy. Cool on a wire rack. Remove the paper cases.

4 For the filling, whip the cream and peppermint extract until stiff. Fit a small, plain nozzle into a piping bag and spoon in the cream. Press the nozzle into the bottom of a cake. Squeeze in 15ml/1 tbsp of the cream. Repeat with the remaining cakes.

5 To make the glaze, melt the chocolate and butter in a pan over low heat, stirring. Stir in the peppermint.

6 Allow to cool, then spread over the cakes.

NUTRITIONAL INFORMATION: Energy 438kcal/1829kJ; Protein 5.1g; Carbohydrate 42.5g, of which sugars 30.3g; Fat 28.7g, of which saturates 17.5g; Cholesterol 101mg; Calcium 82mg; Fibre 1.2g; Sodium 171mg

Fruity Chocolate Cakes

This combination of light sponge, fruity preserve and dark chocolate makes irresistible eating.

ingredients

MAKES EIGHTEEN

- 90g/3½oz/½ cup caster (superfine) sugar
- 2 eggs
- 50g/2oz/½ cup plain (all-purpose) flour
- 75g/3oz/6 tbsp orange marmalade or apricot jam
- 125g/4¼oz plain (semisweet) chocolate

cook's tip

Use lemon curd and top the cakes with a mixture of soft cheese, lemon rind and a little icing (confectioners') sugar to make cheesecake sponges.

1 Preheat the oven to 190°C/375°F/Gas 5. Grease 18 patty tins (muffin pans), preferably non-stick. (If you don't have that many patty tins, you'll need to bake the cakes in batches.)

2 Stand a mixing bowl in very hot water for a couple of minutes to heat through, keeping the inside of the bowl dry. Put the sugar and eggs in the bowl and whisk with a hand-held electric mixer until light and frothy and the beaters leave a trail.

3 Sift the flour over the mixture and stir in gently using a large metal spoon.

4 Divide the mixture among the patty tins. Bake for about 10 minutes, until just firm and pale golden around the edges. Using a palette knife or metal spatula, lift from the tins and transfer to a wire rack to cool.

5 Press the marmalade or jam through a sieve (strainer) to remove any rind or fruit pieces. Spoon a little of the smooth jam on to the centre of each cake.

6 Break the chocolate into small pieces and place in a heatproof bowl set over a pan of gently simmering water. Heat the chocolate, stirring frequently, until it is melted and smooth.

7 Spoon a little chocolate on to the top of each cake and spread gently to the edges with a palette knife. Once the chocolate has just started to set, very gently press it with the back of a fork to give a textured surface. Leave to set for at least 1 hour.

NUTRITIONAL INFORMATION: Energy 84kcal/353kJ; Protein 1.3g; Carbohydrate 14.7g, of which sugars 12.5g; Fat 2.6g, of which saturates 1.3g; Cholesterol 22mg; Calcium 12mg; Fibre 0.3g; Sodium 11mg.

Blueberry Muffins

Light and fruity, these well-known American muffins are delicious at any time of day.

cook's tip

The dry ingredients can be mixed a day ahead and chilled.

1 Preheat the oven to 200°C/400°F/Gas 6. Grease a 12-cup muffin tin (pan) or arrange 12 paper muffin cases on a baking tray.

variation

Use different fruit. Replace the blueberries with the same weight of bilberries, blackcurrants, stoned (pitted) cherries or raspberries. Halved gooseberries, stoned and diced nectarines, plums or peaches are also good.

2 Sift the flour, sugar, baking powder and salt into a large mixing bowl. In another bowl, whisk the eggs until blended. Add the melted butter, milk, vanilla and lemon rind to the eggs, and stir thoroughly to combine.

3 Make a well in the dry ingredients and pour in the egg mixture. With a large metal spoon, stir the flour into the liquid ingredients until the mixture is just moistened, but not smooth. It is important not to overmix muffin batter.

4 Add the blueberries to the muffin mixture and gently fold in, being careful not to crush the berries. Spoon the batter into the muffin tin or paper cases, leaving enough room for the muffins to rise.

5 Bake for 20–25 minutes, until the muffins are set, brown and springy. Leave the muffins in the tin, if using, for 5 minutes before turning them out on to a wire rack to cool slightly. Serve warm.

NUTRITIONAL INFORMATION: Energy 129kcal/543kJ; Protein 3.1g; Carbohydrate 19.6g, of which sugars 7.6g; Fat 4.8g, of which saturates 2.6g; Cholesterol 41mg; Calcium 47mg; Fibre 0.8g; Sodium 44mg.

Butterscotch Nut Muffins

Paper cases are best to prevent these gooey muffins from sticking – they are a real treat.

ingredients

MAKES NINE TO TWELVE

- 150g/5oz butterscotch sweets (candies)
- 225g/8oz/2 cups plain (all-purpose) flour
- 90g/3½oz/7 tbsp golden caster (superfine) sugar
- 10ml/2 tsp baking powder
- 2.5ml/½ tsp salt
- 1 large (US extra large) egg, beaten
- 150ml/¼ pint/⅔ cup milk
- 50ml/2fl oz/¼ cup sunflower oil or melted butter
- 75g/3oz/¾ cup chopped hazelnuts
- butter for greasing, if needed

1 Preheat the oven to 200°C/400°F/Gas 6. Line a 9–12-cup muffin tin (pan) with paper cases or grease with butter.

2 With floured fingers, break the butterscotch sweets into small chunks; alternatively, roughly chop them using a heavy knife. You can toss the sweets in a little flour, if necessary, to prevent them from sticking together.

3 Sift the flour, sugar, baking powder and salt together into a large bowl.

4 Gently whisk the egg with the milk and oil or butter, then stir this into the bowl with the dry ingredients.

5 Add the sweets and nuts and fold the ingredients into the batter. Do not overmix – there should still be a few lumps of flour in the mixture.

6 Spoon the mixture into the prepared muffin tins, filling the paper cases about half full. Bake for about 20 minutes, until well risen, springy and golden brown.

7 Cool the muffins in the tin for 5 minutes, then transfer them to a cooling rack. As with all quick cakes, these are best eaten the same day.

cook's tip

For a special treat, try spreading these muffins with a little Spanish dulce de leche (available from larger supermarkets); it is rather like sweetened condensed milk that has been boiled in the can until caramelized.

NUTRITIONAL INFORMATION: Energy 224kcal/941kJ; Protein 3.9g; Carbohydrate 31.7g, of which sugars 14.6g; Fat 10g, of which saturates 2.1g; Cholesterol 19mg; Calcium 66mg; Fibre 1g; Sodium 55mg.

Double Chocolate Chip Muffins

These muffins are packed with chunky dark and white chocolate chips and dusted with cocoa.

ingredients

MAKES SIXTEEN

- 400g/14oz/3½ cups plain (all-purpose) flour
- 15 – l/1 tbsp baking powder
- 30 – l/2 tbsp unsweetened cocoa powder, plus extra for dusting
- 115g/4oz/¾ cup dark muscovado (molasses) sugar
- 2 eggs
- 150ml/¼ pint/⅔ cup sour cream
- 150ml/¼ pint/⅔ cup milk
- 60ml/4 tbsp sunflower oil
- 75g/6oz white chocolate
- 75g/6oz plain (semisweet) chocolate

1 Preheat the oven to 190°C/375°F/Gas 5. Place 16 paper muffin cases in muffin tins (pans) or deep patty tins. Sift the flour, baking powder and cocoa powder into a bowl and stir in the sugar. Make a well in the centre.

2 In a separate bowl, beat the eggs with the sour cream, milk and oil, then pour into the well in the centre of the dry ingredients. Beat well, gradually incorporating the flour mixture to make a thick and creamy batter.

3 Chop the white and the plain chocolate into small pieces, then stir into the batter mixture, taking care not to overmix.

4 Spoon the mixture into the muffin cases, filling them almost to the top.

5 Bake for 25–30 minutes, or until well risen and firm to the touch.

6 Allow the muffins to cool on a wire rack, then dust with cocoa powder before serving.

cook's tip

Overmixing the batter knocks out the air and makes the mixture heavy. The odd lump of flour or dry patch of mixture is fine; they absorb moisture and cook out during baking.

NUTRITIONAL INFORMATION: Energy 281kcal/1183kJ; Protein 4.7g; Carbohydrate 41.3g, of which sugars 21.9g; Fat 11.9g, of which saturates 5.7g; Cholesterol 7mg; Calcium 94mg; Fibre 1.3g; Sodium 40mg.

Coconut Coffee Squares

Coconut and coffee are natural partners, as these tempting little squares of iced cake prove.

ingredients

SERVES NINE

- 45ml/3 tbsp ground coffee
- 75ml/5 tbsp near-boiling milk
- 25g/1oz/2 tbsp caster (superfine) sugar
- 175g/6oz/²⁄₃ cup golden (light corn) syrup
- 75g/3oz/6 tbsp butter
- 40g/1½oz/½ cup desiccated (dry unsweetered shredded) coconut
- 175g/6oz/1½ cups plain (all-purpose) flour
- 2.5ml/½ tsp bicarbonate of soda (baking soda)
- 2 eggs, lightly beaten

For the icing

- 115g/4oz/8 tbsp butter, softened
- 225g/8oz/2 cups icing (confectioner's) sugar, sifted
- 25g/1oz/⅓ cup shredded or flaked coconut, toasted

1 Preheat the oven to 160°C/325°F/Gas 3. Grease and line the base of a 20cm/8in square cake tin (pan).

2 Put the ground coffee in a small bowl and pour the hot milk over. Leave to infuse for about 4 minutes, then strain through a fine sieve (strainer).

3 Heat the caster sugar, golden syrup, butter and desiccated coconut in a pan over a low heat, stirring with a wooden spoon, until the butter has completely melted.

4 Sift the flour and bicarbonate of soda together and stir into the mixture with the eggs and 45ml/3 tbsp of the coffee-flavoured milk.

5 Spoon the mixture into the prepared tin and spread it evenly, smoothing the top. Bake for 40–50 minutes, until well risen, firm and springy to the touch.

6 Allow the cake to cool in the tin for about 10 minutes, before running a knife around the edges to loosen. Turn out and cool on a wire rack.

7 To make the icing, beat the softened butter until smooth, then gradually beat in the icing sugar and remaining coffee milk to give a soft consistency.

8 Spread the icing over the cake and decorate with toasted coconut. Cut into 5cm/2in squares to serve.

NUTRITIONAL INFORMATION: Energy 453kcal/1898kJ; Protein 4.2g; Carbohydrate 60g, of which sugars 45.7g; Fat 23.5g, of which saturates 15.3g; Cholesterol 88mg; Calcium 66mg; Fibre 1.6g; Sodium 204mg.

Rainbow Gingerbread Squares

These gingerbread squares are spongy and deliciously spicy with both ground and stem ginger.

ingredients

MAKES SIXTEEN

- 225g/8oz/2 cups plain (all-purpose) flour
- 5ml/1 tsp baking powder
- 10ml/2 tsp ground ginger
- 2 pieces preserved stem ginger from a jar, finely chopped
- 90g/3½oz/¾ cup raisins
- 50g/2oz/¼ cup glacé (candied) cherries, chopped
- 115g/4oz/½ cup unsalted (sweet) butter, diced
- 115g/4oz/⅓ cup golden (light corn) syrup
- 30ml/2 tbsp black treacle (molasses)
- 75g/3oz/⅓ cup dark muscovado (molasses) sugar
- 2 eggs, beaten

For the decoration

- 200g/7oz/1¾ cups icing (confectioners') sugar
- 50g/2oz/¼ cup unsalted (sweet) butter, at room temperature, diced
- multi-coloured sprinkles

1 Preheat the oven to 160°C/ 325°F/Gas 3. Line and grease a 20cm/8in square shallow baking tin (pan).

2 Sift the flour, baking powder and ground ginger into a bowl. Add the stem ginger, raisins and cherries and stir together well.

3 Put the butter, syrup, treacle and muscovado sugar in a small pan and heat gently until the butter melts. Pour the mixture into the dry ingredients. Add the eggs and stir well until evenly combined.

4 Tip the mixture into the baking tin and spread evenly. Bake for about 55 minutes, or until risen and firm in the centre. Leave to cool in the tin.

5 To make the topping, put the icing sugar and butter in a bowl. Beat in 20ml/4 tsp hot water until smooth, creamy and just thin enough to pour.

6 Turn the gingerbread out of the baking tin on to a board. Using a large, sharp knife, carefully cut the gingerbread into 16 squares.

7 Drizzle a thick line of icing around the top edge of each square. Don't worry if it falls down the sides. Scatter the sprinkles over the icing to finish and leave to set.

NUTRITIONAL INFORMATION: Energy 251kcal/1057kJ; Protein 2.4g; Carbohydrate 41.9g, of which sugars 31.1g; Fat 9.4g, of which saturates 5.6g; Cholesterol 46mg; Calcium 50mg; Fibre 0.6g; Sodium 100mg.

Almond Cakes

These firm biscuit-like cakes have a fabulous flavour of macaroons and marzipan.

ingredients

SERVES SIXTEEN

- 350g/12oz/3 cups ground almonds
- 50g/2oz/½ cup matzo meal
- 1.5ml/¼ tsp salt
- 30ml/2 tbsp vegetable oil
- 250g/9oz/1¼ cups sugar
- 300g/11oz/1⅓ cups brown sugar
- 3 eggs, separated
- 7.5ml/1½ tsp almond extract
- 5ml/1 tsp vanilla extract
- 150ml/¼ pint/⅔ cup orange juice
- 150ml/¼ pint/⅔ cup brandy
- 200g/7oz/1¾ cups icing (confectioners') sugar

1 Preheat the oven to 180°C/350°F/Gas 4. Lightly grease a 30–38cm/12–15in square cake tin (pan).

2 Put the ground almonds, matzo meal and salt in a bowl and mix together.

3 Put the oil, sugars, egg yolks, almond extract, vanilla extract, orange juice and half the brandy in a separate bowl. Stir well, then add the almond mixture and fold it in to form a thick batter, which may appear slightly lumpy.

4 Whisk the egg whites until stiff. Stir in one-third of the egg whites into the mixture to lighten it, then fold in the rest. Pour the mixture into the prepared tin, spread evenly and bake for 25–30 minutes.

5 Meanwhile, mix the remaining brandy with the icing sugar. If necessary, add a little water to make an icing (frosting) with the consistency of single (light) cream. Remove the cake from the oven and prick the top all over with a skewer or fork.

6 Pour the icing over the top of the cake, then return to the oven for a further 10 minutes, or until the top is crusty.

7 Leave the cake to cool in the tin. Cut it into squares to serve.

NUTRITIONAL INFORMATION: Energy 415kcal/1742kJ; Protein 7.6g; Carbohydrate 54g, of which sugars 51g; Fat 17.9g, of which saturates 1.7g; Cholesterol 36mg; Calcium 97mg; Fibre 2.1g; Sodium 21mg.

Cheesecake Brownies

This dense chocolate brownie mixture is swirled with creamy cheese to give a marbled effect.

ingredients

MAKES SIXTEEN

For the cheesecake mixture

• 1 egg
• 225g/8oz/1 cup cream cheese
• 50g/2oz/¼ cup caster (superfine) sugar
• 5ml/1 tsp vanilla extract

For the brownie mixture

• 115g/4oz dark (bittersweet) chocolate
• 115g/4oz/½ cup unsalted (sweet) butter
• 150g/5oz/¾ cup light muscovado (brown) sugar
• 2 eggs, beaten
• 50g/2oz/½ cup plain (all-purpose) flour

1 Preheat the oven to 160°C/325°F/Gas 3. Line the base and sides of a 20cm/8in cake tin (pan) with baking parchment.

2 To make the cheesecake mixture, beat the egg in a mixing bowl, then add the cream cheese, caster sugar and vanilla extract. Beat together until smooth and creamy.

3 To make the brownie mixture, melt the chocolate and butter together in the microwave or in a heatproof bowl over a pan of water.

4 When the chocolate mixture has melted, remove the bowl from the heat and stir well, until the butter and chocolate are smooth. Then stir in the sugar. Add the eggs, a little at a time, and beat well. Gently stir in the flour.

5 Spread two-thirds of the brownie mixture over the base of the tin.

6 Spread the cheesecake mixture on top, then spoon on the remaining brownie mixture in heaps.

7 Using a skewer, swirl the two mixtures together.

8 Bake the brownies for 30 minutes, or until risen and just set in the centre. Leave to cool in the tin, then cut into squares before serving.

NUTRITIONAL INFORMATION: Energy 226kcal/940kJ; Protein 2.4g; Carbohydrate 20.1g, of which sugars 17.7g; Fat 15.7g, of which saturates 9.4g; Cholesterol 65mg; Calcium 34mg; Fibre 0.3g; Sodium 100mg.

Butterscotch Brownies

These irresistible sticky treats are made with brown sugar, white chocolate chips and walnuts.

ingredients

MAKES TWELVE

- 450g/1lb white chocolate chips
- 75g/3oz/6 tbsp unsalted (sweet) butter
- 3 eggs
- 175g/6oz/¾ cup light muscovado (brown) sugar
- 175g/6oz/1½ cups self-raising (self-rising) flour
- 175g/6oz/1½ cups walnuts, chopped
- 5ml/1 tsp vanilla extract

cook's tip

For a healthier version, use 115g/4oz dark (bittersweet) chocolate chips instead of white ones. Add a peeled, grated large carrot and a peeled, cored and grated apple with the grated rind of 1 orange and 115g/4oz chopped dried apricots.

1 Preheat the oven to 190°C/375°F/Gas 5. Line the base of a 28 x 18cm/11 x 7in baking tin (pan) with baking parchment. Lightly grease the sides.

2 Melt 90g/3½oz of the chocolate chips with the butter in a bowl set over a pan of hot water. Leave to cool slightly.

3 Put the eggs and light muscovado sugar into a large bowl and whisk well until thoroughly combined, then whisk in the melted chocolate mixture.

4 Sift in the flour into the bowl and gently fold it in along with the chopped walnuts, vanilla extract and the remaining chocolate chips.

5 Pour the mixture into the prepared tin and spread evenly.

6 Bake for about 30 minutes, or until risen and golden brown. The centre should be firm to the touch but it will be slightly soft until the brownies cool.

7 Leave to cool completely in the tin, then cut into 12 equal bars.

NUTRITIONAL INFORMATION: Energy 469kcal/1961kJ; Protein 8.1g; Carbohydrate 48.7g, of which sugars 37.7g; Fat 28.3g, of which saturates 11.4g; Cholesterol 61mg; Calcium 182mg; Fibre 1g; Sodium 151mg.

White Chocolate Brownies

These irresistible brownies are rich and luscious with creamy white chocolate and juicy dried fruit.

ingredients

MAKES EIGHTEEN

- 400g/14oz white chocolate, chopped
- 75g/3oz/6 tbsp unsalted (sweet) butter, diced
- 3 eggs
- 90g/3½oz/½ cup golden caster (superfine) sugar
- 10ml/2 tsp vanilla extract
- 90g/3½oz/¾ cup sultanas (golden raisins)
- coarsely grated rind of 1 lemon, plus 15ml/1 tbsp juice
- 200g/7oz/1¾ cups plain (all-purpose) flour

cook's tip

When melting chocolate, avoid getting water into the bowl or the chocolate will separate.

1 Preheat the oven to 190°C/ 375°F/Gas 5. Grease and line a 28 x 20cm/11 x 8in shallow baking tin (pan) with baking parchment.

2 Melt 300g/11oz of the chocolate with the butter in a bowl over a pan of simmering water, stirring frequently.

3 Remove from the heat and beat in the eggs and sugar until thoroughly combined. Add the vanilla extract, sultanas, lemon rind and juice, flour and the remaining chocolate.

4 Thoroughly mix the ingredients, stirring with a wooden spoon, then spread the mixture in the tin. Bake the brownie mixture for about 20 minutes until slightly risen and just golden. The centre should still be slightly soft.

5 Allow to cool completely in the tin. Cut into small squares and carefully remove from the tin.

NUTRITIONAL INFORMATION: Energy 232kcal/973kJ; Protein 4g; Carbohydrate 30.3g, of which sugars 21.8g; Fat 11.4g, of which saturates 6.5g; Cholesterol 41mg; Calcium 86mg; Fibre 0.4g; Sodium 65mg.

Tuscan Citrus Sponge

This cake traditionally comes from the little Tuscan town of Pitigliano, in Italy.

ingredients

SERVES SIX TO EIGHT

- 12 eggs, separated
- 300g/11oz/1½ cups caster (superfine) sugar
- 120ml/4fl oz/½ cup fresh orange juice
- grated rind of 1 orange
- grated rind of 1 lemon
- 50g/2oz/½ cup potato flour, sifted
- 90g/3½oz/¾ cup fine matzo meal or matzo meal flour, sifted
- large pinch of salt
- icing (confectioners') sugar, for dusting (optional)

1 Preheat the oven to 160°C/ 325°F/Gas 3. Whisk the egg yolks until pale and frothy, then whisk in the sugar, orange juice, orange and lemon rind.

2 Fold the sifted flours into the egg mixture.

3 In a large bowl, whisk the egg whites with the salt until they are stiff, then fold them into the egg yolk mixture.

4 Carefully pour the cake mixture into a deep, ungreased 25cm/10in cake tin (pan).

5 Bake the cake in the oven for about 1 hour, or until it is well risen, springy to touch and golden. Leave to cool in the tin.

6 When cold, turn out the cake and invert it on to a serving plate. Dust with a little icing sugar before serving, if you wish.

cook's tip

This tangy sponge makes a good dessert, especially when served with a refreshing fruit salad and whipped cream.

NUTRITIONAL INFORMATION: Energy 328kcal/1381kJ; Protein 11.1g; Carbohydrate 53.7g, of which sugars 40.5g; Fat 8.8g, of which saturates 2.3g; Cholesterol 285mg; Calcium 66mg; Fibre 0.4g; Sodium 109mg.

Italian Zucotto

This Italian-style dessert has a rich ricotta, fruit and nut filling encased in moist, chocolate cake.

ingredients

SERVES EIGHT

- 3 eggs
- 75g/3oz/6 tbsp caster (superfine) sugar
- 75g/3oz/¾ cup plain (all-purpose) flour
- 25g/1oz/¼ cup unsweetened cocoa powder, plus extra, for dusting
- 90ml/6 tbsp Kirsch
- 250g/9oz/generous 1 cup ricotta cheese
- 50g/2oz/½ cup icing (confectioners') sugar
- 50g/2oz plain (semisweet) chocolate, finely chopped
- 50g/2oz/½ cup blanched almonds, chopped and toasted
- 75g/3oz/scant ½ cup natural glacé cherries, quartered
- 2 pieces preserved stem ginger, finely chopped
- 150ml/¼ pint/⅔ cup double (heavy) cream

1 Preheat the oven to 180°C/ 350°F/Gas 4. Line and grease a 23cm/9in cake tin (pan). Whisk the eggs and sugar in a bowl until very thick and pale.

2 Sift the flour and cocoa powder into the bowl and fold it in with a large metal spoon. Spoon the mixture into the prepared tin and bake for about 20 minutes, until just firm. Cool.

3 Cut the cake into three layers. Set aside 30ml/2 tbsp of the Kirsch. Drizzle the rest over the layers.

4 Beat the ricotta, then beat in the icing sugar, chocolate, almonds, cherries, ginger and reserved Kirsch.

5 Whip the cream and fold it into the ricotta mixture. Chill. Cut and set aside a 20cm/8in circle from one cake layer.

6 Cut the remaining cake to line a 3.4-litre/6-pint/15-cup freezerproof bowl. Cut a circle for the base and pieces for the sides, fitting them together to about one-third of the way up the sides of the bowl.

7 Spoon the filling into the bowl to the top of the sponge. Lay the circle of sponge on top, trim the edges and cover. Freeze overnight.

8 Transfer to the refrigerator 45 minutes before serving, to soften slightly Turn on to a plate, dust with cocoa powder and serve.

NUTRITIONAL INFORMATION: Energy 391kcal/1631kJ; Protein 8.7g; Carbohydrate 33.8g, of which sugars 26.1g; Fat 22.7g, of which saturates 11.4g; Cholesterol 111mg; Calcium 66mg; Fibre 1.3g; Sodium 64mg.

Spanish Biscocho Borracho

The name of this moist dessert translates as "drunken cake", indicating that it is soaked in brandy.

ingredients

SERVES SIX TO EIGHT

- 6 large (US extra large) eggs, separated
- 90g/3½oz/½ cup caster (superfine) sugar
- finely grated rind of 1 lemon
- 90g/3½oz/¾ cup plain (all-purpose) flour, sifted twice
- 90ml/6 tbsp toasted flaked almonds
- 250ml/8fl oz/1 cup whipping cream, to serve

For the syrup

- 115g/4oz/generous ½ cup caster (superfine) sugar
- 120ml/4fl oz/½ cup boiling water
- 105ml/7 tbsp Spanish brandy

1 Preheat the oven to 200°C/400°F/Gas 6. Line and grease a shallow tin (pan), about 28 x 18cm/11 x 7in.

2 Beat the egg yolks with the sugar and lemon rind until light. Whisk the whites to soft peaks, then work a little white into the yolks. Drizzle two spoonfuls of yolk mixture across the whites, sift some flour over the top and cut in gently with a spoon.

3 Continue folding in the yolk mixture and flour until both have been incorporated.

4 Turn the mixture into the tin. Bake for 12 minutes. Leave to set for 5 minutes, then turn out on to a wire rack. Peel off the paper and leave to cool.

5 To make the syrup, heat 50g/2oz/¼ cup sugar in a small pan with 15ml/1 tbsp water until it caramelizes. As soon as it colours, dip the base of the pan into cold water. Add the remaining sugar and boiling water. Simmer, stirring until the sugar has dissolved. Pour into a jug (pitcher) and add the brandy.

6 Put the cake back into the tin and drizzle over half the syrup. Scoop the cake into scallops with a spoon and layer half in a 700ml/1½ pint/3 cup capacity mould or tin. Scatter 30ml/2 tbsp almonds over and push them down the cracks. Top with the remaining cake and 30 ml/2 tbsp nuts.

7 Pour the remaining syrup over, and cover with foil. Weight down the top and chill. Run a knife round the mould and turn out. Scatter with almonds and serve with cream.

NUTRITIONAL INFORMATION: Energy 294kcal/1235kJ; Protein 8.3g; Carbohydrate 36.3g, of which sugars 27.4; Fat 10.6g, of which saturates 1.7g; Cholesterol 143mg; Calcium 78mg; Fibre 1.2g; Sodium 56mg.

Portuguese Sponge Cake

A very popular sponge, this cake is distinctive for its especially moist centre.

Ingredients

SERVES SIX

- melted butter, for brushing
- 125g/4¼oz/generous 1 cup plain (all-purpose) flour
- 5 eggs
- 12 egg yolks
- 240g/8½oz/generous 2 cups icing (confectioner's) sugar

For the cinnamon sauce

- 105ml/7 tbsp milk
- 45ml/3 tbsp icing (confectioner's) sugar
- 2 egg yolks
- pinch of ground cinnamon

1 Preheat the oven to 160°C/325°F/Gas 3. Brush a round cake tin (pan), 20cm/8in in diameter and 5cm/2in deep, with melted butter. Line with baking parchment and brush with melted butter again.

2 Sift the flour into a bowl and set aside. Beat the eggs and yolks with the sugar in another bowl until light and fluffy. Gradually fold in the flour.

3 Spoon the mixture into the prepared tin and bake for 25 minutes. Leave to cool.

4 Meanwhile, make the cinnamon sauce. Put all the ingredients in a heatproof bowl. Set the bowl over a pan of simmering water and beat well until slightly thickened. Taste and beat in more cinnamon if required. Leave to cool.

5 To serve, remove the cake from the tin, using the baking parchment to ease it out.

6 Cut the cake into equal slices, bearing in mind that the centre is moist, and place on individual plates. Serve with the cinnamon sauce spooned over the top.

variation

Melt 125g/4¼oz of dark (bittersweet) chocolate and 125g/4¼oz of butter, and fold into the mixture at the end of step 2 to produce a delightful chocolate sponge.

NUTRITIONAL INFORMATION: Energy 485kcal/2041kJ; Protein 15.8g; Carbohydrate 67.4g, of which sugars 51.5g; Fat 18.9g, of which saturates 5.4g; Cholesterol 662mg; Calcium 159mg; Fibre 0.7g; Sodium 102mg.

Austrian Sachertorte

This glorious gateau was created in Vienna in 1832 by Franz Sacher, a chef in the royal household.

ingredients

SERVES TEN TO TWELVE

- 225g/8oz dark (bittersweet) chocolate, broken into squares
- 150g/5oz/⅔ cup unsalted (sweet) butter, softened
- 115g/4oz/½ cup caster (superfine) sugar
- 8 eggs, separated
- 115g/4oz/1 cup plain (all-purpose) flour, sifted

For the glaze

- 225g/8oz/1 cup apricot jam
- 15ml/1 tbsp lemon juice

For the icing

- 225g/8oz dark (bittersweet) chocolate, broken into squares
- 200g/7oz/scant 1 cup caster (superfine) sugar
- 15ml/1 tbsp golden (light corn) syrup
- 250ml/8fl cz/1 cup double (heavy) cream
- 5ml/1 tsp vanilla extract
- plain (semisweet) chocolate curls, to decorate

1 Preheat the oven to 180°C/350°F/Gas 4. Line and grease a 23cm/9in round springform cake tin (pan). Melt the chocolate in a heatproof bowl set over a pan of barely simmering water, stirring occasionally until smooth.

2 Cream the butter and sugar until pale and fluffy, then beat in the egg yolks, one at a time, and the melted chocolate. Fold in the flour.

3 Whisk the egg whites in a separate, perfectly clean bowl until stiff.

4 Stir a quarter of the whites into the chocolate mixture. Fold in the remaining whites. Tip into the tin and level the top. Bake for 50–55 minutes, until firm, then turn out on to a wire rack to cool.

5 For the glaze, heat the jam with the lemon juice in a pan until melted, then strain into a bowl. Slice the cold cake in half across the middle to make two layers. Brush the top and sides of each layer with the glaze, then sandwich them together. Place on a wire rack.

6 Heat all the icing ingredients gently, stirring, until thick and smooth. Simmer for 3–4 minutes to 95°C/200°F on a sugar thermometer. Pour over the cake and spread evenly. Decorate with curls.

NUTRITIONAL INFORMATION: Energy 581kcal/2425kJ; Protein 50.5g; Carbohydrate 29.1g, of which sugars 11.2g; Fat 26.5g, of which saturates 7.4g; Cholesterol 224mg; Calcium 109mg; Fibre 6.9g; Sodium 668mg.

Greek Semolina Cake

This is a family treat, loved by everyone in Greece. It is economical and takes very little time to make.

ingredients

SERVES SIX TO EIGHT

- 500g/1¼lb/2¾ cups caster (superfine) sugar
- 1 litre/1¾ pints/4 cups cold water
- 1 cinnamon stick
- 250ml/8fl oz/1 cup olive oil
- 350g/12oz/2 cups coarse semolina
- 50g/2oz/½ cup blanched almonds
- 30ml/2 tbsp pine nuts
- 5ml/1 tsp ground cinnamon

1 Put the sugar in a large, heavy pan. Carefully pour in the water and then add the cinnamon stick.

2 Bring to the boil, stirring continuously, until the sugar dissolves, then boil without stirring for 4 minutes to make a syrup.

3 Heat the oil in a heavy pan until it is almost smoking. Then add the semolina gradually to the pan and keep stirring until it is lightly browned.

4 Lower the heat, add the almonds and pine nuts, and brown for 2–3 minutes, stirring.

5 Set the semolina mixture aside off the heat. Remove the cinnamon from the syrup using a slotted spoon and discard it.

6 Protecting your hand with an oven glove, add the hot syrup to the semolina mixture a little at a time, stirring continuously.

7 Return the pan to a gentle heat and stir until all the syrup has been absorbed and the mixture looks smooth.

8 Remove from the heat, cover with a clean dish towel and allow to stand for 10 minutes so any remaining moisture is absorbed.

9 Scrape the mixture into a 20cm/3in round cake tin (pan), preferably fluted, and set it aside. When it is cold, transfer to a serving platter and dust it with the ground cinnamon. Cut into slices to serve.

NUTRITIONAL INFORMATION: Energy 888kcal/3,731kJ; Protein 9.1g; Carbohydrate 133.1g, of which sugars 87.6g; Fat 39.1g, of which saturates 4.9g; Cholesterol 0mg; Calcium 75mg; Fibre 1.9g; Sodium 13mg.

Greek Lemon and Lime Cake

This Greek favourite is perfect for busy cooks as it can be mixed in moments and needs no icing.

ingredients

SERVES EIGHT

- 5ml/1 tsp baking powder
- 225g/8oz/2 cups self-raising (self-rising) flour
- 225g/8oz/generous 1 cup caster (superfine) sugar
- 225g/8oz/1 cup butter, softened
- 4 eggs, beaten
- grated rind of 2 lemons
- 30ml/2 tbsp lemon juice

For the topping

- finely pared rind of 1 lime
- juice of 2 limes
- 150g/5oz/⅔ cup caster (superfine) sugar

1 Preheat the oven to 160°C/325°F/Gas 3. Grease and line a 20cm/8in round tin (pan).

2 Sift the baking powder and flour into a bowl. Add the sugar, butter, eggs, lemon rind and juice and beat well.

3 Spoon the mixture into the prepared tin, then smooth the surface and make a shallow indentation in the top with the back of a spoon.

4 Bake for 1½ hours, or until the cake is golden and a skewer inserted into the centre comes out clean.

variation

Use the rind and juice of one large lemon instead of lime for the topping, if you prefer.

5 Mix the topping ingredients together in a small bowl. As soon as the cake is cooked, remove it from the oven and pour the topping evenly over the surface. Allow the cake to cool in the tin, then remove and cut into slices to serve.

NUTRITIONAL INFORMATION: Energy 524kcal/2197kJ; Protein 6g; Carbohydrate 70.4g, of which sugars 49.5g; Fat 26.2g, of which saturates 15.5g; Cholesterol 155mg; Calcium 143mg; Fibre 0.9g; Sodium 310mg.

Norwegian Almond Cake

Almonds are popular throughout Scandinavia and this cake uses them in an irresistible topping.

ingredients

SERVES TEN

- 50g/2oz/4 tbsp unsalted (sweet) butter
- 115g/4oz/1 cup plain (all-purpose) flour
- 7.5ml/1½ tsp baking powder
- pinch of salt
- 2 large eggs
- 150g/5oz/¾ cup caster (superfine) sugar

For the topping

- 115g/4oz/½ cup butter, softened
- 150g/5oz/1½ cups blanched almonds, toasted and roughly chopped
- 115g/4oz/generous ½ cup caster (superfine) sugar
- 30ml/2 tbsp plain (all-purpose) flour
- 30ml/2 tbsp single (light) cream or milk

1 Preheat the oven to 160°C/325°F/Gas 3. Line and grease a 20cm/8in round cake tin (pan). Melt the butter and leave to cool. Sift together the flour, baking powder and salt.

2 In a large bowl, whisk the eggs until thick and pale. Gradually whisk in the sugar until the mixture falls in a thick ribbon. Fold in the flour mixture and the cooled butter.

3 Pour the mixture into the prepared tin and tap lightly on a work surface.

4 Bake the cake for 30 minutes, or until almost cooked – firm to the touch but in need of another few minutes to prevent it from sinking if removed from the heat.

5 Leave the cake in the oven and prepare the topping. Place the butter, almonds, sugar, flour and cream or milk in a pan and heat gently, stirring, until the butter has melted. Continue heating the mixture until it just reaches boiling point, stirring all the time to prevent it from becoming lumpy.

6 Preheat the grill (broiler) to medium-hot. Remove the cake from the oven and spread the topping over it.

7 Grill (broil) until golden, watching that the sides don't burn. Stand the tin on a rack so that air can pass underneath, and cool before removing the cake from the tin.

NUTRITIONAL INFORMATION: Energy 389kcal/1626kJ; Protein 6.1g; Carbohydrate 40.2g, of which sugars 28.7g; Fat 23g, of which saturates 10g; Cholesterol 75mg; Calcium 82mg; Fibre 1.5g; Sodium 119mg

Finnish Spice Cake

Spices elevate Finland's plain cakes and bakes, creating delicious and aromatic results.

ingredients

MAKES ONE CAKE

- 225g/8oz butter, plus extra for greasing
- 4 eggs
- 225g/8oz/generous 1 cup caster (superfine) sugar
- 5ml/1 tsp ground cardamom
- 5ml/1 tsp ground cinnamon
- 5ml/1 tsp ground ginger
- 15ml/1 tbsp grated orange rind
- 2.5ml/½ tsp bicarbonate of soda (baking soda)
- 300ml/½ pint/1¼ cups sour cream
- 225g/8oz/2 cups plain (all-purpose) flour

1 Preheat the oven to 200°C/400°F/Gas 6. Grease a 23cm/9in loose-bottomed cake tin (pan) with butter. Melt the remaining butter.

2 Put the eggs and sugar in a large bowl and whisk until light and fluffy. Add the cardamom, cinnamon, ginger and grated orange rind and stir together.

3 In a separate bowl, mix the bicarbonate of soda into the sour cream, then add to the egg mixture.

4 Add the flour to the bowl and mix in thoroughly. Pour the mixture into the prepared tin and bake in the oven for about 1 hour, or until it is risen, set and browned. The cake should feel springy to the touch.

5 Cool in the tin for 10 minutes, turn on to a wire rack, remove the tin and cool completely.

cook's tips

• *Single (light) cream can be substituted for the sour cream but you should then replace the bicarbonate of soda with 5ml/1 tsp baking powder.*

• *If you have a kugelhopf mould, then this can be used to give the finished cake a more interesting shape.*

NUTRITIONAL INFORMATION: Energy 3379kcal/14025kJ; Protein 57.7g; Carbohydrate 191.1g, of which sugars 16.1g; Fat 271.1g, of which saturates 161.5g; Cholesterol 1421mg; Calcium 767mg; Fibre 7g; Sodium 1777mg.

Hungarian Fruit Bread

This recipe produces a lovely, light, white cake which keeps very well, if tightly wrapped.

ingredients

SERVES EIGHT TO TEN

- 7 egg whites
- 175g/6oz/generous ¾ cup caster (superfine) sugar
- 115g/4oz/1 cup flaked almonds, toasted
- 115g/4oz/¾ cup sultanas (golden raisins)
- grated rind of 1 lemon
- 160g/5½oz/1⅓ cups plain (all-purpose) flour, sifted, plus extra for flouring
- 75g/3oz/6 tbsp unsalted (sweet) butter, melted

cook's tip

To ensure that the fruit loaf stays especially moist, you can wrap it closely in cling film (plastic wrap) while it is still warm and allow to cool completely. Then store the loaf in the refrigerator until it is required.

1 Preheat the oven to 180°C/ 350°F/Gas 4 and grease and flour a 1kg/2¼lb loaf tin (pan).

2 Whisk the egg whites until stiff, but not dry. Fold in the sugar, then the almonds, sultanas and lemon rind.

3 Fold the flour and butter into the egg whites. Tip the mixture into the tin and spread it evenly into the corners.

4 Bake the loaf for about 45 minutes, until well risen and pale golden brown.

5 Allow the loaf to cool slightly for a few minutes in the tin, then carefully turn it out. The fruit loaf can be served either warm or cold. If serving cold, turn it out of the tin and leave to cool on a wire rack.

NUTRITIONAL INFORMATION: Energy 289kcal/1216kJ; Protein 6.4g; Carbohydrate 39.5g, of which sugars 27g; Fat 12.8g, of which saturates 4.5g; Cholesterol 16mg; Calcium 69mg; Fibre 1.6g; Sodium 93mg.

Polish Apple Cake

This cake is firm and moist, with pieces of apple peeking through the golden crust.

ingredients

SERVES SIX TO EIGHT

- 375g/13oz/3½ cups self-raising (self-rising) flour
- 3–4 large cooking apples, or cooking and eating apples
- 10ml/2 tsp ground cinnamon
- 500g/1¼ b/2½ cups caster (superfine) sugar
- 4 eggs, lightly beaten
- 250ml/8fl oz/1 cup vegetable oil
- 120ml/4fl oz/½ cup orange juice
- 10ml/2 tsp vanilla extract
- 2.5ml/½ tsp salt

cook's tip

Using orange juice instead of milk is typical of Jewish baking as it allows the cake to be eaten with both meat and dairy meals.

1 Preheat the oven to 180°C/350°F/Gas 4. Grease a 30 x 38cm/12 x 15in square cake tin (pan) and dust with flour.

2 Core and thinly slice the apples using a sharp knife, but do not peel them.

3 Put the sliced apples in a bowl and mix with the cinnamon and 75ml/5 tbsp of the sugar.

4 In a separate bowl, beat the eggs, remaining sugar, vegetable oil, orange juice and vanilla extract together until combined. Sift in the remaining flour and salt, then stir into the mixture.

5 Pour two-thirds of the cake mixture into the prepared tin, top with one-third of the apples, then pour over the remaining cake mixture.

6 Top the cake with the remaining apple and bake for about 1 hour, or until risen, set and golden brown.

7 Leave the cake to cool in the tin to allow the juices to soak in.

8 Cut the apple cake into small squares, and serve while still warm.

NUTRITIONAL INFORMATION: Energy 653kcal/2751kJ; Protein 7.8g; Carbohydrate 105.4g, of which sugars 70.6g; Fat 25.3g, of which saturates 3.4g; Cholesterol 95mg; Calcium 215mg; Fibre 2.1g; Sodium 210mg.

Polish Coffee and Almond Torte

Roasted almonds give this Polish cake, a coffee-filled sponge, a rich and nutty flavour.

ingredients

SERVES EIGHT TO TEN

- 75g/3oz/½ cup blanched almonds
- 225g/8oz/1 cup butter, softened
- 225g/8oz/generous 1 cup caster (superfine) sugar
- 4 eggs, beaten
- 150g/5oz/1¼ cups self-raising (self-rising) flour, sifted

For the icing

- 175g/6oz/1 cup blanched almonds
- 40g/1½oz/9 tbsp ground coffee
- 75ml/5 tbsp near-boiling water
- 150g/5oz/¾ cup caster (superfine) sugar
- 30ml/6 tbsp water
- 3 egg yolks
- 225g/8oz/1 cup unsalted (sweet) butter, well beaten

1 Preheat the oven to 190°C/375°F/Gas 5. Base line and grease three 3 x 18cm/7in round sandwich tins (pans).

2 Put the almonds on a baking sheet and roast for 7 minutes, or until golden brown. Allow to cool, then process until fine in a food processor.

3 Cream the butter and sugar together in a bowl until pale and fluffy. Gradually add the eggs, beating well after each addition. Fold in the ground almonds and the flour.

4 Divide the mixture evenly among the three tins and bake for 25–30 minutes, until well risen and firm to the touch. Turn out and cool on a wire rack.

5 To make the icing, put the blanched almonds in a bowl and pour over enough boiling water to cover. Allow to cool, then drain and cut each nut into 4 or 5 slivers. Roast on a baking sheet for 8 minutes.

6 Put the ground coffee in a jug (pitcher), spoon over the water and leave to stand.

7 Dissolve the sugar in 90ml/6 tbsp water. Simmer for 3 minutes, to 107°C/225°F on a sugar thermometer. Whisk the egg yolks, pouring in the syrup until thick. Beat this into the butter. Strain the coffee and beat into the icing. Use to sandwich the cakes together and over the top. Press in the almond slivers and cut into slices to serve.

NUTRITIONAL INFORMATION: Energy 765kcal/3184kJ; Protein 12g; Carbohydrate 52.5g, of which sugars 40.7g; Fat 57.9g, of which saturates 26.5g; Cholesterol 340mg; Calcium 171mg; Fibre 2.3g; Sodium 368mg.

62

Russian Poppy Seed Cake

Black poppy seeds give this cake its nutty, distinctive taste that is utterly delicious.

ingredients

SERVES EIGHT

- 130g/4½oz/generous 1 cup self-raising (self-rising) flour
- 5ml/1 tsp baking powder
- 2.5ml/½ tsp salt
- 2 eggs
- 225g/8oz/generous 1 cup caster (superfine) sugar
- 5–10ml/1–2 tsp vanilla extract
- 200g/7oz/scant 1½ cups poppy seeds, ground
- 15ml/1 tbsp grated lemon rind
- 120ml/4fl oz/½ cup milk
- 130g/4½oz/generous ½ cup unsalted (sweet) butter, melted and cooled
- 30ml/2 tbsp vegetable oil
- icing (confectioners') sugar, sifted, for dusting

1 Preheat the oven to 180°C/350°F/Gas 4. Line the base of a 23cm/9in springform tin (pan) and grease. In a bowl, sift together the flour, baking powder and salt.

2 Using an electric whisk, beat together the eggs, sugar and vanilla extract for 4–5 minutes until pale and fluffy. Stir in the poppy seeds and lemon rind.

3 Fold the sifted ingredients into the mixture, in three batches and alternating with the milk.

4 Fold in the melted butter and vegetable oil. Pour the mixture into the tin and bake for 40 minutes, or until firm.

5 Cool the cake in the tin for 15 minutes, then invert the cake on to a wire rack to cool.

6 When the poppy seed cake is completely cool, dust generously with icing sugar and cut into wedges before serving.

variation

To make a poppy seed tart, pour the cake mixture into a par-cooked pastry crust, then bake for 30 minutes.

NUTRITIONAL INFORMATION: Energy 485kcal/2023kJ; Protein 8.3g; Carbohydrate 42.7g, of which sugars 30.5g; Fat 32.4g, of which saturates 11.4g; Cholesterol 83mg; Calcium 267mg; Fibre 2.5g; Sodium 188mg.

Mexican Garbanzo Cake

This moist cake has a pudding-like texture. It tastes wonderful with mango or pineapple and yogurt.

ingredients

SERVES SIX

- 2 x 275g/10oz cans chickpeas, drained
- 4 eggs, beaten
- 225g/8oz/1 cup caster superfine sugar
- 5ml/1 tsp baking powder
- 10ml/2 tsp ground cinnamon
- grated rind and juice of 1 orange

For the cinnamon sugar

- 50g/2oz/¼ cup caster superfine sugar
- 5ml/1tsp ground cinnamon

1 Preheat the oven to 180°C/350°F/Gas 4.

2 Tip the chickpeas into a colander, drain thoroughly, and pour into a bowl. Rub them between your hands to remove the skins.

3 Transfer to a food processor and process to a smooth purée.

4 Spoon the purée into a bowl and stir in the eggs, sugar, baking powder, cinnamon, orange rind and juice. Grease and line a 450g/1lb loaf tin (pan).

5 Pour the cake mixture into the loaf tin, level the surface and bake for about 1½ hours or until a skewer inserted into the centre comes out clean.

6 Remove from the oven and leave to cool, in the tin, for 10 minutes. Remove from the tin and place on a wire rack.

7 To make the cinnamon sugar, mix 50g/2oz/¼ cup caster sugar with 5ml/1 tsp ground cinnamon. Sprinkle the cinnamon sugar over the top of the cake.

8 Leave the cake to cool completely. Cut into slices and serve with sliced fresh pineapple.

NUTRITIONAL INFORMATION: Energy 344kcal/1455kJ; Protein 14.1g;
Carbohydrate 57.9g, of which sugars 39.1g; Fat 7.9g, of which saturates 1.6g;
Cholesterol 152mg; Calcium 104mg; Fibre 5.3g; Sodium 325mg.

Middle Eastern Kodafa

Throughout the Middle East, kodafa are made in trays and carried through the streets on sellers' heads.

ingredients

SERVES SIX

- 250g/9oz/1½ cups couscous
- 500ml/17fl oz/2¼ cups boiling water
- 200g/7oz/scant 1 cup butter, cut into small pieces
- 1 egg, lightly beaten
- pinch of salt
- 400g/14oz/1¾ cups ricotta cheese
- 200g/7oz cheese, such as mozzarella, Taleggio or Monterey Jack, grated or finely chopped
- 350ml/12fl oz/1½ cups clear honey
- 2–3 pinches of saffron threads or ground cinnamon
- 120ml/4fl oz/½ cup water
- 5ml/1 tsp orange flower water or lemon juice
- 90ml/6 tbsp roughly chopped shelled pistachio nuts

1 Put the couscous in a bowl and pour over the boiling water. Stir with a fork, then leave to soak for about 30 minutes until the water is absorbed.

2 When the couscous is cool enough to handle, break up all the lumps with your fingers. Stir the butter into the couscous, then stir in the egg and salt.

3 Preheat the oven to 200°C/400°F/Gas 6. Spread half the couscous into a 30cm/12in round cake tin (pan).

4 In a bowl, combine the cheeses and 30ml/2 tbsp of the honey. Spread on top of the couscous, then top with the remaining couscous. Press down gently and evenly and bake for 10–15 minutes.

5 Meanwhile, put the remaining honey, the saffron threads or cinnamon, and the water in a pan. Bring to the boil, then boil for 5–7 minutes, or until the liquid forms a syrup. Remove from the heat and stir in the orange flower water or lemon juice.

6 When the kodafa is cooked, place under a hot grill (broiler) and cook until the top of the cake is lightly browned to a golden crust.

7 Sprinkle the pistachio nuts all over the top of the kodafa. Serve warm, cut into wedges, with the honey syrup.

NUTRITIONAL INFORMATION: Energy 702kcal/2927kJ; Protein 17.6g; Carbohydrate 65.1g, of which sugars 47.6g; Fat 43g, of which saturates 22.7g; Cholesterol 123mg; Calcium 140mg; Fibre 0.9g; Sodium 344mg.

Moroccan Yogurt Cake

In Morocco this type of moist cake isn't necessarily reserved for dessert – it is enjoyed at any time of day.

ingredients

SERVES FOUR TO SIX

- 3 eggs, separated
- 75g/3oz/scant ½ cup caster (superfine) sugar
- seeds from 2 vanilla pods (beans)
- 300ml/½ pint/1¼ cups Greek (US strained plain) yogurt
- grated rind and juice of 1 lemon
- scant 15ml/1 tbsp plain (all-purpose) flour
- handful of pistachio nuts, roughly chopped
- 90ml/6 tbsp crème fraîche and 6 fresh passion fruit or 50g/2oz/½ cup summer berries, to serve

1 Preheat the oven to 180°C/350°F/Gas 4. Line a 25cm/10in square, ovenproof dish with baking parchment and grease well.

2 Beat the egg yolks with two-thirds of the sugar, until pale and fluffy. Beat in the vanilla seeds and then stir in the yogurt, lemon rind and juice. Stir in the flour.

3 Whisk the egg whites until stiff, then gradually whisk in the rest of the sugar to form soft peaks.

4 Fold the whisked whites into the yogurt mixture. Turn the cake mixture into the lined dish and spread it out evenly.

5 Place the dish in a roasting pan with cold water to come about halfway up the outside of the dish. This prevents the cake from baking too quickly.

6 Bake for about 20 minutes until the mixture is risen and just set. Sprinkle the pistachio nuts over the cake and cook for a further 20 minutes, until browned on top.

7 Serve the cake warm or chilled with crème fraîche and a spoonful of passion fruit drizzled over the top. Alternatively, sprinkle with a few summer berries such as redcurrants, blackcurrants and blueberries.

cook's tip

When whisking egg whites, all equipment must be completely grease-free. Any trace of egg yolk in the whites will prevent them from retaining the air.

NUTRITIONAL INFORMATION: Energy 152kcal/638kJ; Protein 6.6g; Carbohydrate 16g, of which sugars 14.1g; Fat 7.9g, of which saturates 3.4g Cholesterol 95mg; Calcium 99mg; Fibre 0.1g; Sodium 71mg.

Iced Strawberry Gateau

Make this lemon and strawberry flavoured dessert the day before a summer party.

ingredients

SERVES EIGHT

- 115g/4oz/½ cup unsalted (sweet) butter, softened
- 115g/4oz/generous ½ cup caster (superfine) sugar
- 2 eggs
- 115g/4oz/1 cup self-raising (self-rising) flour
- 2.5ml/½ tsp baking powder

To finish

- 500ml/17fl oz/2¼ cups strawberry ice cream
- 300ml/½ pint/1¼ cups double (heavy) cream
- 200g/7oz/scant 1 cup good-quality lemon curd
- 30ml/2 tbsp lemon juice
- 500g/1¼lb/5 cups strawberries, hulled
- 25g/1oz/2 tbsp caster (superfine) sugar
- 45ml/3 tbsp Cointreau or other orange-flavoured liqueur

1 Preheat the oven to 180°C/ 350°F/Gas 4. Line and grease a 23cm/9in round springform tin (pan). In a mixing bowl, beat the butter with the sugar, eggs, flour and baking powder until creamy.

2 Spoon the mixture into the prepared tin, spread it out evenly and bake for about 20 minutes, or until just firm. Leave to cool for 5 minutes, then turn the cake out on a wire rack. Cool completely. Wash and dry the cake tin, ready to use again.

3 Line the sides of the clean cake tin with a strip of non-stick baking parchment. Trim off the top of the cake where it has formed a crust.

4 Fit the cake into the tin, cut-side down. Freeze for 10 minutes, then spread the ice cream evenly over the cake and freeze until firm.

5 Whip the cream until it forms soft peaks, then fold in the lemon curd and lemon juice. Spoon this over the strawberry ice cream. Freeze overnight.

6 Decorate the cake about 45 minutes before serving it. Slice half the strawberries. Put the rest in a food processor or blender and add the sugar and liqueur. Purée the mixture.

7 Arrange sliced strawberries over the gateau. Serve with the sauce spooned over.

NUTRITIONAL INFORMATION: Energy 653kcal/2725kJ; Protein 6.5g; Carbohydrate 66.8g, of which sugars 49.9g; Fat 40.2g, of which saturates 24.6g; Cholesterol 150mg; Calcium 164mg; Fibre 1.2g; Sodium 224mg.

Raspberry Mousse Gateau

A lavish quantity of raspberries gives this gateau its vibrant colour and full flavour.

ingredients

SERVES EIGHT TO TEN

- 2 eggs
- 50g/2oz/¼ cup caster (superfine) sugar
- 50g/2oz/½ cup plain (all-purpose) flour
- 30ml/2 tbsp unsweetened cocoa powder
- 500g/1lb 5oz/3½ cups raspberries
- 115g/4oz/1 cup icing (confectioners') sugar
- 30ml/4 tbsp whisky (optional)
- 300ml/½ pint/1¼ cups whipping cream
- 2 egg whites

1 Preheat the oven to 180°C/ 350°F/Gas 4. Line and grease a 23cm/9in springform tin (pan). Whisk the eggs and sugar in a heatproof bowl set over a pan of gently simmering water until the whisk leaves a trail when lifted. Remove the bowl from the heat and continue to whisk for 2 minutes.

2 Sift the flour and cocoa powder over the mixture and fold it in with a metal spoon. Spoon the mixture into the tin and spread it out. Bake for 12–15 minutes, until firm.

3 Cool, then remove the cake from the tin and place on a wire rack. Wash and dry the tin.

4 Line the sides of the clean tin with a strip of baking parchment and carefully lower the cake back into it. Freeze until the raspberry filling is ready.

5 Set aside 200g/7oz/generous 1 cup of the raspberries. Put the remainder in a clean bowl, stir in the icing sugar, process to a purée in a food processor or blender. Strain into a bowl, then stir in the whisky, if using.

6 Whip the cream to form soft peaks. Whisk the egg whites until they are stiff. Using a large metal spoon, fold the cream, then the egg whites, into the raspberry purée.

7 Spread half the raspberry mixture over the cake. Scatter with the reserved raspberries. Spread the remaining raspberry mixture on top. Cover and freeze the gateau overnight.

8 Transfer the gateau to the refrigerator at least 1 hour before serving. Remove it from the tin, place on a serving plate and serve in slices.

NUTRITIONAL INFORMATION: Energy 238kcal/996kJ; Protein 4.4g; Carbohydrate 25g, of which sugars 20.9g; Fat 14.1g, of which saturates 8.3g; Cholesterol 70mg; Calcium 58mg; Fibre 2g; Sodium 65mg.

Exotic Celebration Gateau

Use any tropical fruits you can find for a spectacular display of colours and tastes for this confection.

ingredients

MAKES ONE 20cm/8in RING GATEAU

- 175g/6oz/¾ cup butter, softened
- 175g/6oz/scant 1 cup caster (superfine) sugar
- 3 eggs, beaten
- 250g/9oz/2¼ cups self-raising (self-rising) flour
- 30–45ml/2–3 tbsp milk
- 90–120ml/6–8 tbsp light rum

For the decoration

- 400ml/14fl oz/1⅔ cups double (heavy) cream
- 25g/1oz/¼ cup icing (confectioners') sugar, sifted
- 450g/1lb mixed fresh exotic and soft fruits, such as figs, redcurrants, star fruit (carambola) and kiwi fruit
- 90ml/6 tbsp apricot jam, warmed and strained
- 30ml/2 tbsp warm water
- icing (confectioners') sugar

1 Preheat the oven to 190°C/375°F/Gas 5. Grease and flour a deep 20cm/8in ovenproof ring mould.

2 Beat together the butter and sugar until light and fluffy. Gradually beat in the eggs, then fold in the flour and milk.

cook's tip

The cake can be baked several days in advance and stored in an airtight container in the refrigerator.

3 Spoon the mixture into the ring mould. Level the top. Bake the cake for 45 minutes, or until a skewer inserted into the centre comes out clean. Turn out on to a wire rack and leave to cool completely.

4 Place the cake on a serving plate. Make holes randomly over the cake with a skewer. Drizzle over the rum and allow it to soak in.

5 To make the icing, beat the cream and icing sugar until the mixture holds soft peaks.

6 Spread the icing all over the cake. Arrange the fruits in the hollow centre of the cake.

7 To make a glaze, mix the apricot jam and warm water together in a small pan and heat, stirring, until combined. Brush this over the fruit. Sift with icing sugar to finish.

NUTRITIONAL INFORMATION: Energy 5783kcal/24084kJ; Protein 57.2g;
Carbohydrate 481.4g, of which sugars 289.6g; Fat 394.7g, of which saturates 238.5g;
Cholesterol 1528mg; Calcium 933mg; Fibre 16.3g; Sodium 1428mg.

Maple and Nut Meringue Gateau

This simple dessert makes a feast for all meringue lovers. Before serving, let it thaw slightly.

ingredients

SERVES TEN TO TWELVE

- 4 egg whites
- 200g/7oz/scant 1 cup light muscovado sugar
- 150g/5oz/1¼ cups walnut pieces
- 600ml/1 pint/2½ cups double (heavy) cream
- 150ml/¼ pint/⅔ cup maple syrup plus extra, to serve

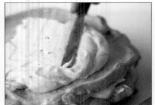

1 Preheat the oven to 140°C/275°F/Gas 1. Draw three 23cm/9in circles on separate sheets of baking parchment.

2 Invert the sheets on three baking sheets. Whisk the egg whites in a grease-free bowl until stiff.

cook's tip

Always use fresh egg whites when making meringues. Old egg whites don't rise well in the oven.

3 Whisk in the sugar, 15ml/1 tbsp at a time, whisking well after each addition until the meringue is stiff and glossy. Spread to within 1cm/½in of the edge of each marked circle. Bake for about 1 hour or until crisp. Leave to cool.

4 Set aside 45ml/3 tbsp of the walnuts. Finely chop the rest. Whip the cream with the maple syrup until it forms soft peaks. Fold in the chopped walnuts. Use a third of the mixture to sandwich the meringues together on a serving plate.

5 Using a palette knife or metal spatula, spread the remaining cream mixture over the top and sides of the gateau. Sprinkle with the reserved walnuts and freeze overnight.

6 Transfer the gateau to the refrigerator about 1 hour before serving so that the cream filling softens slightly.

7 Drizzle a little of the extra maple syrup over the top of the gateau just before serving. Cut into slices to serve.

NUTRITIONAL INFORMATION: Energy 441kcal/1831kJ; Protein 3.7g; Carbohydrate 28.6g, of which sugars 28.5g; Fat 35.4g, of which saturates 17.4g; Cholesterol 69mg; Calcium 48mg; Fibre 0.4g; Sodium 67mg.

Tia Maria Gateau

A feather-light coffee sponge, this has a creamy liqueur-flavoured filling spiked with stem ginger.

ingredients

SERVES EIGHT

- 75g/3oz/¾ cup plain (all-purpose) flour
- 30ml/2 tbsp instant coffee powder
- 3 eggs
- 115g/4oz/½ cup caster (superfine) sugar

For the filling

- 175g/6oz/generous ¾ cup low-fat soft cheese
- 15ml/1 tbsp clear honey
- 15ml/1 tbsp Tia Maria
- 50g/2oz/⅓ cup preserved stem ginger, chopped

For the icing

- 225g/8oz/2 cups icing (confectioners') sugar, sifted
- 10ml/2 tsp coffee extract
- 5ml/1 tsp unsweetened cocoa powder
- coffee beans

1 Preheat the oven to 190°C/375°F/Gas 5. Line and grease a 20cm/8in round cake tin (pan). Sift the flour and coffee together into a bowl.

2 Whisk the eggs and sugar in a bowl until thick and mousse-like, then fold in the flour mixture lightly.

3 Turn the mixture into the prepared tin. Bake for 30–35 minutes, or until the cake is risen, firm and golden. It should feel springy to the touch. Cool on a wire rack.

4 To make the coffee-cheese filling, mix the soft cheese with the honey in a bowl. Beat until smooth, then stir in the Tia Maria and preserved stem ginger. Slice the cake in half horizontally and sandwich it back together with the Tia Maria filling.

5 To make the icing, mix the icing sugar and coffee extract in a bowl. Stir in enough water to make an icing that will coat the back of a wooden spoon. Pour three-quarters of the icing over the cake.

6 Stir the cocoa powder into the remaining icing until smooth and evenly combined. Spoon this mocha icing into a piping (icing) bag fitted with a writing nozzle.

7 Drizzle the mocha icing over the coffee icing. Decorate with coffee beans, and leave until set. Store in an airtight container in the refrigerator. Remove 30 minutes before serving.

NUTRITIONAL INFORMATION: Energy 247kcal/1050kJ; Protein 4.9g; Carbohydrate 54.7g, of which sugars 47.4g; Fat 2.5g, of which saturates 1.5g; Cholesterol 12mg; Calcium 65mg; Fibre 0.5g; Sodium 120mg.

Classic Creamy Cheesecake

This classic version of fruit cheesecake is simple, sophisticated and superbly tempting.

ingredients

SERVES SIX TO EIGHT

- 130g/4½oz/generous ½ cup unsalted (sweet) butter, melted
- 350g/12oz digestive biscuits (graham crackers), finely crushed
- 350–400g/12–14oz/1¾–2 cups caster (superfine) sugar
- 350g/12oz/1½ cups full-fat soft white (farmer's) cheese
- 3 eggs, lightly beaten
- 15ml/1 tbsp vanilla extract
- 350g/12oz/1½ cups sour cream
- mixed berries and icing (confectioners') sugar, to serve (optional)

1 Butter a deep 23cm/9in springform tin (pan). Put the biscuit crumbs and 60ml/4 tbsp of the sugar in a bowl and mix together, then add the melted butter and mix well.

2 Press the mixture into the prepared tin to cover the base and sides. Chill for 30 minutes.

variation

For lemon cheesecake, use the grated rind and juice of 1 lemon instead of vanilla extract.

3 Preheat the oven to 190°C/375°F/Gas 5. Using an electric mixer, food processor or wooden spoon, beat the cheese until soft. Beat in the eggs, then 250g/9oz/1½ cups of the sugar and 10ml/2 tsp of the vanilla extract.

4 Pour the mixture over the crumb base and bake for 45 minutes, or until a cocktail stick (toothpick), inserted in the centre, comes out clean. Leave to cool slightly for about 10 minutes. (Do not turn the oven off.)

5 Meanwhile, combine the sour cream and remaining sugar, to taste. Stir in the remaining vanilla extract. When the cheesecake has cooled, pour over the topping, spreading it out evenly. Return to the oven and bake for a further 5 minutes to glaze.

6 Leave the cheesecake to cool, then chill in the refrigerator. Serve with mixed berries such as strawberries, blueberries and raspberries, dusted with icing sugar, if you like.

NUTRITIONAL INFORMATION: Energy 634kcal/2628kJ; Protein 7.8g; Carbohydrate 31.8g, of which sugars 7.7g; Fat 53.8g, of which saturates 31.5g; Cholesterol 192mg; Calcium 137mg; Fibre 1g; Sodium 536mg.

Lemon and Lime Cheesecake

This tangy cheesecake would be best described as a citrus sensation.

ingredients

MAKES EIGHT SLICES

- 150g/5oz/1½ cups digestive biscuits (graham crackers)
- 40g/1½oz/3 tbsp butter

For the topping

- grated rind and juice of 2 lemons
- 10ml/2 tsp powdered gelatine
- 250g/9oz/generous 1 cup ricotta cheese
- 75g/3oz/6 tbsp caster (superfine) sugar
- 150ml/¼ pint/⅔ cup double (heavy) cream
- 2 eggs, separated

For the lime syrup

- pared rind and juice of 3 limes
- 75g/3oz/6 tbsp caster (superfine) sugar
- 5ml/1 tsp arrowroot mixed with 30ml/2 tbsp water
- green food colouring (optional)

1 Lightly grease a 20cm/8in round springform cake tin (pan). Crush the biscuits finely in a food processor or blender. Melt the butter in a large pan, then stir in the crumbs until well coated. Spoon into the tin, press the crumbs down well in an even layer, then chill.

2 Make the topping. Place the lemon rind and juice in a small pan and sprinkle over the gelatine. Leave for 5 minutes. Heat gently until the gelatine has dissolved, then set aside to cool slightly.

3 Beat the ricotta cheese and sugar in a bowl. Stir in the cream and egg yolks, then whisk in the cooled gelatine mixture.

4 Whisk the egg whites in a grease-free bowl until they form soft peaks. Fold them into the cheese mixture. Spoon on to the biscuit base, level the surface and chill for 2–3 hours.

5 Meanwhile, make the lime syrup. Place the lime rind and juice and sugar in a small pan. Bring to the boil, stirring, then boil the syrup for 5 minutes.

6 Stir the arrowroot mixture into the syrup and continue to stir until the syrup boils and thickens slightly. Remove from the heat immediately. Tint pale green with a food colouring, if you like. Cool, then chill.

7 Spoon the syrup over the cheesecake. Serve sliced.

NUTRITIONAL INFORMATION: Energy 366kcal/1526kJ; Protein 6g; Carbohydrate 33.8g, of which sugars 23.5g; Fat 23.9g, of which saturates 13.8g; Cholesterol 105mg; Calcium 44mg; Fibre 0.4g; Sodium 166mg.

White Chocolate Cheesecake

Raspberries complement this mascarpone and white chocolate mix, on its crunchy ginger and nut base.

ingredients

SERVES EIGHT

- 50g/2oz/4 tbsp unsalted (sweet) butter
- 225g/8oz/2⅓ cups ginger nut biscuits (gingersnaps), crushed
- 50g/2oz/½ cup pecan nuts or walnuts, chopped

For the filling

- 275g/10oz/1¼ cups mascarpone
- 175g/6oz/¾ cup fromage frais or soft white (farmer's) cheese
- 2 eggs, beaten
- 40g/1½oz/3 tbsp caster (superfine) sugar
- 250g/9oz white chocolate, broken into squares
- 225g/8oz/1⅓ cups fresh or frozen raspberries

For the topping

- 115g/4oz/½ cup mascarpone
- 75g/3oz/⅓ cup fromage frais or soft white (farmer's) cheese
- white chocolate curls and raspberries, to decorate

1 Preheat the oven to 150°C/300°F/Gas 2. Melt the butter in a pan, then stir in the crushed biscuits and nuts. Press into the base of a 23cm/9in springform cake tin (pan).

2 Make the filling. Beat the mascarpone and fromage frais, then beat in the eggs and caster sugar until evenly mixed.

3 Melt the white chocolate gently in a heatproof bowl over hot water. Stir the chocolate into the cheese mixture with the raspberries.

4 Turn the mixture into the prepared tin and spread it evenly over the biscuit base, then bake for about 1 hour or until the cheesecake mixture is just set.

5 Switch off the oven, but do not remove the cheesecake. Leave it until cold and firmly set. Then chill lightly.

6 Remove the cheesecake from the tin by unclipping the sides and leaving the base in place. Transfer the cheesecake on its metal base to a serving platter.

7 To make the topping, mix the mascarpone and fromage frais or soft white cheese. Spread this over the cake and top with chocolate curls and fruit.

NUTRITIONAL INFORMATION: Energy 551kcal/2305kJ; Protein 12.8g; Carbohydrate 53.9g, of which sugars 41.4g; Fat 33.1g, of which saturates 17g; Cholesterol 88mg; Calcium 170mg; Fibre 1.4g; Sodium 195mg.

Cranberry and Blueberry Cake

Cranberries have a great flavour and they are perfect with blueberries in sweet cakes of this type.

ingredients

MAKES TEN SLICES

- 175g/6oz/¾ cup unsalted (sweet) butter, softened
- 115g/4oz/½ cup caster (superfine) sugar
- 350g/12oz/3 cups plain (all-purpose) flour
- 2 large eggs, beaten
- 5ml/1 tsp baking powder
- 5ml/1 tsp pure vanilla extract
- 115g/4oz/1 cup cranberries
- 115g/4oz/1 cup blueberries
- 50g/2oz/⅓ cup light muscovado (molasses) sugar
- 2.5ml/½ tsp crushed cardamom seeds
- icing (confectioners') sugar, for dusting

1 Preheat the oven to 190°C/375°F/Gas 5. Line and grease the base of a 21cm/8½in springform tin (pan).

2 Cream the butter and caster sugar together until pale, smooth and light.

3 Rub in the flour with your fingers until the mixture resembles fine breadcrumbs. Take out 200g/7oz/generous 1 cup of this mixture and set it aside for the topping.

4 Beat the eggs, baking powder and vanilla extract into the remaining mixture until soft and creamy. Spoon the mixture into the tin and spread it out evenly. Arrange the cranberries and blueberries in an even layer over the mixture. Then sprinkle the muscovado sugar evenly over the fruit.

5 Stir the cardamom seeds into the reserved flour mixture, then scatter it evenly over the top of the fruit.

6 Bake the cake for 50–60 minutes, or until the topping is golden. Cool the cake in the tin for 10 minutes, then remove the sides of the tin. Slide it on to a wire rack off its base. Cool the cake completely.

7 Dust the top of the cake with icing sugar and serve in slices.

NUTRITIONAL INFORMATION: Energy 342kcal/1436kJ; Protein 5g; Carbohydrate 47.8g, of which sugars 20.2g; Fat 16g, of which saturates 9.5g; Cholesterol 75mg; Calcium 67mg; Fibre 1.5g; Sodium 122mg.

Orange and Almond Cake

The key to this recipe is to cook the orange slowly first, so it is fully tender before being blended.

ingredients

SERVES EIGHT

- 1 large orange
- 3 eggs
- 225g/8oz/1 cup caster (superfine) sugar
- 5ml/1 tsp baking powder
- 225g/8oz/2 cups ground almonds
- 25g/1oz/¼ cup plain (all-purpose) flour
- icing (confectioners') sugar, for dusting
- orange slices (optional), to serve

1 Wash the orange and pierce it with a skewer. Put it in a deep pan and pour over water to cover completely. Bring to the boil, then lower the heat, cover and simmer for 1 hour, or until the skin is very soft. Drain, then cool.

2 Preheat the oven to 180°C/350°F/Gas 4. Grease a 20cm/8in round cake tin (pan) and line it with baking parchment. Halve the orange and discard the pips. Purée the orange (with peel) in a food processor until smooth.

3 Whisk the eggs and sugar until thick. Fold in the baking powder, almonds, flour and purée.

4 Pour the mixture into the prepared tin, level the surface and bake for 1 hour or until risen, browned and firm.

5 If the cake is cooked, a skewer inserted into the middle should come out without any sticky mixture clinging to it.

6 Cool the cake in the tin for 10 minutes, then turn it out on to a wire rack, peel off the lining paper and leave until warm or cool completely.

7 Dust the top of the cake liberally with icing sugar and serve warm, as a dessert.

cook's tip

For colour, tuck slices of orange under the cake before serving.

NUTRITIONAL INFORMATION: Energy 327kcal/1369kJ; Protein 3.9g; Carbohydrate 35g, of which sugars 31.9g; Fat 17.8g, of which saturates 1.8g; Cholesterol 71mg; Calcium 105mg; Fibre 2.4g; Sodium 39mg.

Almond and Raspberry Roll

This light and airy sponge is rolled up with a rich fresh cream and raspberry filling.

ingredients

MAKES ONE 23CM/9IN
LONG ROLL

- 3 eggs
- 75g/3oz/6 tbsp caster (superfine) sugar
- 50g/2oz/½ cup plain (all-purpose) flour, sifted
- 30g/2 tbsp ground almonds
- caster (superfine) sugar, for dusting
- 250ml/8fl oz/1 cup double (heavy) cream
- 225g/8oz/1⅓ cups fresh raspberries
- 16 flaked (sliced) almonds, toasted, to decorate

1 Preheat the oven to 200°C/ 400°F/Gas 6. Grease a 33 x 23cm/13 x 9in Swiss roll tin (jelly roll pan), line with baking parchment and grease the paper.

2 Whisk the eggs and sugar in a heatproof bowl until blended. Place the bowl over a pan of simmering water and whisk until thick and pale.

3 Remove from the heat, then whisk off the heat until cool. Sift over the flour and almonds, and fold in gently.

4 Transfer to the prepared tin and bake for 10–12 minutes, until well risen and springy to the touch.

5 Sprinkle a sheet of baking parchment with caster sugar. Invert the cake on to the paper and leave to cool with the tin still in place. Carefully remove the tin and lining paper.

6 Whip the cream until it holds its shape. Gradually fold in 250g/ 9oz/1¼ cups of the fresh raspberries.

7 Spread the cream and raspberry mixture over the cooled cake with a metal spatula, leaving a narrow border round the edges.

8 Carefully roll up the cake from a narrow end to form a Swiss roll, using the baking parchment to lift the sponge. Sprinkle the roll liberally with caster sugar.

9 Cut into slices and serve with the reserved raspberries and toasted flaked almonds on the side.

NUTRITIONAL INFORMATION: Energy 2166Kcal/9012kJ; Protein 37.3g; Carbohydrate 133.9g, of which sugars 95g; Fat 169g, of which saturates 89.8g; Cholesterol 914mg; Calcium 446mg; Fibre 9.4g; Sodium 282mg.

Ginger Cake

Three types of ginger make this the ultimate cake for all lovers of the versatile spice.

ingredients

MAKES TWELVE SQUARES

- 225g/8 oz/2 cups self-raising (self-rising) flour
- 15ml/1 tbsp ground ginger
- 5ml/1 tsp ground cinnamon
- ½ tsp bicarbonate of soda (baking soda)
- 115g/4 oz/½ cup butter
- 115g/4 oz/½ cup soft light brown sugar
- 2 eggs
- 25ml/1½ tbsp golden (light corn) syrup
- 25ml/1½ tbsp milk

For the topping
- 6 pieces preserved stem ginger, plus 20ml/4 tsp syrup, from the jar
- 115g/4 oz/1 cup icing (confectioners') sugar
- lemon juice

1 Preheat the oven to 160°C/ 325°F/Gas 3. Line and grease a shallow 18cm/7in square cake tin (pan) with baking parchment.

2 Gently sift the flour, ginger, cinnamon and bicarbonate of soda into a large bowl. Rub in the butter, then stir in the sugar.

3 Make a well in the centre of the dry ingredients. In a bowl, whisk together the eggs, syrup and milk. Pour into the dry ingredients and beat until smooth and glossy.

4 Spoon the mixture into the prepared tin and spread it out evenly. Bake the cake for 45–50 minutes, until well risen and firm to the touch. Leave in the tin for 30 minutes, then remove to a wire rack to cool completely.

5 Quarter the ginger pieces and arrange on top of the cake.

6 Sift the icing sugar into a bowl and stir in the ginger syrup with enough lemon juice to make a smooth icing.

7 Put the icing into a baking parchment icing bag and drizzle over the top of the cake. Leave to set, then cut into squares to serve.

NUTRITIONAL INFORMATION: Energy 235kcal/989kJ; Protein 3.3g; Carbohydrate 37g, of which sugars 22.1g; Fat 9.3g, of which saturates 5.3g; Cholesterol 52mg; Calcium 49mg; Fibre 0.6g; Sodium 79mg.

Ginger and Peach Cake

Peaches and peach schnapps are layered in the centre of this moist ginger Madeira cake.

ingredients

SERVES EIGHT

- 225g/8oz/2 cups plain (all-purpose) flour
- 7.5ml/1½ tsp baking powder
- 10ml/2 tsp ground ginger
- 175g/6oz/¾ cup butter
- 175g/6oz/¾ cup caster (superfine) sugar
- 3 eggs, beaten
- 3 fresh peaches, stoned (pitted) and sliced
- 45ml/3 tbsp peach schnapps

For the topping

- 25g/1oz/2 tbsp butter
- 25g/1oz/¼ cup plain (all purpose) flour
- 30ml/2 tbsp caster (superfine) sugar
- 50g/2oz/½ cup flaked (sliced) almonds, crushed

1 Preheat the oven to 180°C/350°F/Gas 4. Line and grease a 20cm/8in springform cake tin (pan).

2 Sift the flour, baking powder and ground ginger into a bowl. In a separate bowl, cream the butter with the sugar until light and fluffy. Beat in the eggs a little at a time.

3 Fold the flour and spices into the creamed mixture until thoroughly mixed. Spoon half the cake mixture into the cake tin.

4 Arrange the peach slices in circles on top. Pour over the peach schnapps and cover with the remaining cake mixture.

5 For the topping, rub the butter into the flour, then stir in the sugar and almonds.

6 Sprinkle the topping over the top of the cake and bake for 1¼–1½ hours, or until cooked. Cool on a wire rack and serve warm or cold.

NUTRITIONAL INFORMATION: Energy 331kcal/1398kJ; Protein 7.5g; Carbohydrate 57.1g, of which sugars 32.2g; Fat 8.9g, of which saturates 2.6g; Cholesterol 78mg; Calcium 91mg; Fibre 2g; Sodium 51mg.

Greek Yogurt and Fig Cake

Baked fresh figs, thickly sliced, make a delectable base for a feather-light sponge.

ingredients

SERVES SIX TO EIGHT

- 8 firm fresh figs, thickly sliced
- 45ml/3 tbsp clear honey, plus extra for glazing cooked figs
- 200g/7oz/scant 1 cup butter, softened
- 175g/6oz/¾ cup caster (superfine) sugar
- grated rind of 1 lemon
- grated rind of 1 orange
- 4 eggs, separated
- 225g/8oz/2 cups plain (all-purpose) flour
- 5ml/1 tsp baking powder
- 5ml/1 tsp bicarbonate of soda (baking soda)
- 250ml/8fl oz/1 cup Greek (US strained plain) yogurt

1 Preheat the oven to 180°C/ 350°F/Gas 4. Line and grease a 23cm/9in cake tin with baking parchment. Arrange the fig slices evenly over the base of the tin and drizzle the honey evenly over them to coat them lightly.

2 In a large bowl, cream the butter and caster sugar with the lemon and orange rinds until pale and fluffy, then gradually beat in the egg yolks.

3 Sift the dry ingredients together. Beat a little into the creamed mixture. Beat in a spoonful of yogurt. Repeat until all the dry ingredients and yogurt are added.

4 Whisk the egg whites until they form stiff peaks. Stir half the whites into the cake mixture to slacken it slightly.

5 Fold in the remaining egg whites and pour the mixture over the figs in the tin. Bake for 1¼ hours, until golden and a skewer inserted into the centre of the cake comes out clean. Turn out on to a wire rack peel off the lining paper and cool. Drizzle the figs with extra honey before serving.

cook's tip

Use firm, ripe figs so that they will retain their shape.

NUTRITIONAL INFORMATION: Energy 473kcal/1981kJ; Protein 8.2g; Carbohydrate 53.7g, of which sugars 40.5g; Fat 8.8g, of which saturates 2.3g; Cholesterol 285mg; Calcium 66mg; Fibre 0.4g; Sodium 109mg.

Coffee Almond Marsala Slice

Roasted and crushed coffee beans are speckled throughout this delicious almond cake.

ingredients

SERVES TEN TO TWELVE

- 25g/1oz/⅓ cup roasted coffee beans
- 5 eggs, separated
- 175g/6oz/scant 1 cup caster (superfine) sugar
- 120ml/4fl oz/½ cup Marsala wine
- 75g/3oz/6 tbsp butter, melted and cooled
- 115g/4oz/1 cup ground almonds
- 115g/4oz/1 cup plain (all-purpose) flour, sifted
- 25g/1oz/¼ cup flaked (sliced) almonds
- icing (confectioners') sugar, to dust
- crème fraîche, to serve

1 Preheat the oven to 180°C/ 350°F/Gas 4. Line and grease the base of a 23cm/9in round loose-based tin (pan).

2 Put the coffee beans on to a large baking sheet and roast for 10 minutes in the oven. Allow to cool, place in a plastic bag and crush with a rolling pin.

3 Put the egg yolks and 115g/ 4oz/generous ½ cup of the caster sugar in a large bowl and beat together until very pale and thick.

4 Stir in the crushed coffee, Marsala, butter and almonds. Sift the flour over, then fold in.

5 Whisk the egg whites until they are stiff, then gradually incorporate the remaining caster sugar.

6 Fold the whites into the almond mixture. Spoon into the tin and sprinkle with flaked almonds. Bake for 10 minutes, then reduce the oven to 160°C/ 325°F/Gas 3 and cook for a further 40 minutes, or until a skewer inserted into the centre comes out clean.

7 Leave the cake to cool in the tin for 5 minutes, then turn it out to cool on a wire rack. Dust with icing sugar and serve cut into wedges, with dollops of crème fraîche.

NUTRITIONAL INFORMATION: Energy 252kcal/1055kJ; Protein 6.1g; Carbohydrate 24.2g, of which sugars 16.6g; Fat 14.1g, of which saturates 4.4g; Cholesterol 93mg; Calcium 63mg; Fibre 1.2g; Sodium 71mg.

Cappuccino Torte

The famous coffee beverage with cream, chocolate and cinnamon makes a sensational dessert.

ingredients

SERVES SIX TO EIGHT

- 75g/3oz/6 tbsp unsweetened (sweet) butter, melted
- 275g/10oz shortbread biscuits, crushed
- 1.5ml/1/4 tsp ground cinnamon
- 25ml/1½ tbsp powdered gelatine
- 45ml/3 tbsp cold water
- 2 eggs, separated
- 115g/4oz/½ cup soft light brown sugar
- 115g/4oz plain (semisweet) chocolate, chopped
- 175ml/6fl oz/¾ cup hot brewed espresso
- 400ml/14fl oz/1⅔ cups whipping cream
- chocolate curls and ground cinnamon to decorate

1 Mix the butter with the biscuits and cinnamon. Spoon into the base of a 20cm/8in loose-based tin (pan) and press down well. Chill while making the filling.

2 Sprinkle the gelatine over the cold water. Leave to soften for 5 minutes, then place the bowl over a pan of hot water and stir to dissolve.

3 Whisk the egg yolks and sugar until thick. Put the chocolate in a bowl. Add the coffee and stir to melt.

4 Add the chocolate and coffee to the egg mixture, then cook gently in a pan for 1–2 minutes, until thickened. Stir in the gelatine. Leave until just beginning to set, stirring occasionally.

5 Whip 150ml/1/4 pint/ 2/3 cup of the cream until soft peaks form. In a separate bowl, whisk the egg whites until stiff. Fold the cream into the coffee mixture, followed by the egg whites. Pour the mixture over the biscuit base and chill for 2 hours.

6 When ready to serve, remove the torte from the tin and cut into slices. Whip the remaining cream and place a dollop on top of each slice. Decorate with chocolate curls and a little cinnamon.

cook's tip

Sprinkling gelatine over water is known as sponging – the gelatine absorbs the water.

NUTRITIONAL INFORMATION: Energy 584kcal/2429kJ; Protein 5.5g;
Carbohydrate 47.3g, of which sugars 30.8g; Fat 42.7g, of which saturates 26.3g;
Cholesterol 146mg; Calcium 81mg; Fibre 1g; Sodium 181mg.

Rice Cake with Fresh Fruit

This is not a dry snack from the health food shop, but a sumptuous celebration gateau.

ingredients

SERVES EIGHT TO TEN

- 225g/8oz/generous 1 cup Thai fragrant rice, rinsed
- 1 litre/1¾ pints/4 cups milk
- 115g/4oz/scant ½ cup caster (superfine) sugar
- 6 green cardamom pods, crushed
- 2 bay leaves
- 300ml/½ pint/1¼ cups whipping cream
- 6 eggs, separated
- red and white currants, sliced star fruit and kiwi fruit, to decorate

For the topping
- 250ml/8fl oz/1 cup double (heavy) cream
- 150g/5oz/⅔ cup Quark or low-fat soft cheese
- 5ml/1 tsp vanilla extract
- grated rind of 1 lemon
- 40g/1½oz/3 tbsp caster (superfine) sugar

1 Line and grease a 25cm/10in round, deep cake tin (pan).

2 Cook the rice in a pan of boiling unsalted water for 3 minutes, then drain, return to the pan and pour in the milk. Stir in the caster sugar, cardamoms and bay leaves. Bring to the boil, then lower the heat and simmer the rice for 20 minutes, stirring occasionally.

3 Remove from the heat and allow the mixture to cool. Then remove the bay leaves and cardamom husks.

4 Preheat the oven to 180°C/350°F/Gas 4. Spoon the rice mixture into a bowl. Beat in the cream and then the egg yolks. Whisk the egg whites until they form soft peaks, then fold them into the rice mixture.

5 Spoon into the prepared tin and bake for 45–50 minutes, until risen and golden. Chill overnight. Turn the cake out on to a large serving plate.

6 Whip the cream until stiff. Gently fold in the Quark, vanilla, lemon rind and sugar.

7 Cover the top of the cake with the cream mixture, spreading it evenly and then swirling it attractively. When ready to serve, decorate the cake with sprigs of red and white currants, slices of star fruit and peeled and sliced kiwi fruit.

NUTRITIONAL INFORMATION: Energy 501kcal/208.46kJ; Protein 11.5g; Carbohydrate 40.1g, of which sugars 22.1g; Fat 33.4g, of which saturates 19.6g; Cholesterol 193mg; Calcium 206.6mg; Fibre 0g; Sodium 107.4mg.

Strawberry Cream Sponge

This is a classic summer treat with soft fruit or with the new season's jam.

ingredients

SERVES EIGHT TO TEN

- 4 eggs
- 115g/4oz/generous ½ cup caster (superfine) sugar, plus extra for dusting
- 90g/3½oz/¾ cup plain (all-purpose) flour, sifted, plus extra for dusting
- icing (confectioners') sugar for dusting

For the filling

- 300ml/½ pint/1¼ cups double (heavy) cream
- about 5ml/1 tsp icing (confectioners') sugar, sieved
- 450g/1 lb/4 cups strawberries, washed and hulled
- a little Cointreau

1 Preheat the oven to 190°C/375°F/Gas 5. Grease a loose-based 20cm/8in deep cake tin (pan), and dust it with 5ml/1 tsp caster sugar mixed with 5ml/1 tsp flour. Shake off any excess sugar and flour.

2 Whisk the eggs and sugar together in a bowl with an electric mixer until light and thick, and the mixture leaves a trail as it drops from the whisk. For speed, set the bowl over a pan a quarter filled with hot water and whisk until thick and creamy.

3 Sift the flour evenly over the eggs and fold it in thoroughly with a metal spoon, losing as little volume as possible.

4 Pour the mixture into the prepared cake tin. Level off the top and bake in the preheated oven for 25–30 minutes, or until the sponge feels springy.

5 Leave in the tin for 1–2 minutes to allow the cake to cool a little and shrink slightly from the sides, then loosen the sides gently with a knife and turn out on to a rack to cool.

6 For the filling, whip the cream with the icing sugar. Slice the sponge in two and spread some cream over the cut sides.

7 Reserve some strawberries, then slice the rest. Arrange the sliced strawberries on the cream. Sprinkle with liqueur, if using. Cover with the second cake layer and press down.

8 Spread the remaining cream on top of the cake, and arrange the reserved strawberries on top. Dust with icing sugar and serve as a dessert.

NUTRITIONAL INFORMATION: Energy 333kcal/1387kJ; Protein 5.3g; Carbohydrate 27.8g, of which sugars 19.2g; Fat 23.1g, of which saturates 13.3g; Cholesterol 147mg; Calcium 65mg; Fibre 1g; Sodium 48mg.

Christmas Panforte

This spicy, sweet treat is very rich, so cut small wedges – offer a glass of sparkling wine to go with it.

ingredients

SERVES TWELVE TO FOURTEEN

- 175g/6oz/1 cup hazelnuts, roughly chopped
- 75g/3oz/½ cup whole almonds, roughly chopped
- 225g/8oz/1⅓ cups mixed candied fruits, diced
- 1.5ml/¼ tsp ground coriander
- 4ml/¾ tsp ground cinnamon
- 1.5ml/¼ tsp ground cloves
- 1.5ml/¼ tsp grated nutmeg
- 50g/2oz/½ cup plain (all-purpose) flour
- 115g/4oz/⅓ cup honey
- 115g/4oz/generous 1 cup sugar
- icing (confectioners') sugar, for dusting

1 Preheat the oven to 180°C/350°F/Gas 4. Grease and line the base of a 20cm/8in round cake tin (pan) with baking parchment.

2 Spread the nuts on a baking tray and bake for 10 minutes, or until lightly toasted. Set aside. Lower the oven temperature to 150°C/300°F/Gas 2.

3 In a large mixing bowl, combine the candied fruits, all the spices and the flour and stir together. Add the nuts and stir in thoroughly.

4 In a small heavy pan, stir the honey and sugar, and bring to the boil. Cook the mixture until it reaches 138°C/280°F on a sugar thermometer or until a little of the mixture forms a hard ball when pressed between fingertips in iced water. Take care when doing this, using a teaspoon to remove a little mixture from the pan.

5 Immediately pour the syrup into the dry ingredients and stir well until evenly mixed. Pour into the prepared tin.

6 Dip a metal spoon into water and use the back of the spoon to press the mixture down in the tin, until evenly thick and smooth on top.

7 Bake for 1 hour. When ready, the panforte will still feel quite soft but it hardens as it cools.

8 Cool in the tin. Turn out on to a plate or wrap tightly in clear film (plastic wrap) and store for up to 2 weeks in an airtight container. Dust with icing sugar to serve.

NUTRITIONAL INFORMATION: Energy 227kcal/955kJ; Protein 3.8g; Carbohydrate 30g, of which sugars 26.6g; Fat 11.1g, of which saturates 0.8g; Cholesterol 0mg; Calcium 53mg; Fibre 1.7g; Sodium 11mg.

Christmas Cake

Bake this cake a month in advance, then add a fruit and nut topping two weeks before Christmas.

ingredients

MAKES ONE 20cm/8in ROUND
OR 18cm/7in SQUARE CAKE

- 225g/8oz/2 cups plain (all-purpose) flour
- 7.5ml/1½ tsp mixed (apple pie) spice
- 900g/2lb/5 cups mixed dried fruit
- 50g/2oz/½ cup slivered almonds
- 115g/4oz/⅔ cup glacé (candied) cherries, halved
- 115g/4oz/⅔ cup chopped mixed (candied) peel
- 225g/8oz/1 cup unsweetened (sweet) butter, at room temperature
- 225g/8oz/1 cup soft dark brown sugar
- 15ml/1 tbsp black treacle (molasses)
- finely grated rind of 1 orange
- 5ml/1 tsp vanilla extract
- 4 large (US extra large) eggs
- 150ml/¼ pint/⅔ cup whisky

1 Line and grease a 20cm/8in round or an 18cm/7in square loose-bottomed cake tin (pan), extending it 5cm/2in above the rim. Tie a thick band of folded newspaper or brown paper around the outside of the tin.

2 Sift the flour and spice into a bowl. Mix the dried fruit with the almonds, cherries, mixed peel and 15ml/1 tbsp of the sifted flour and spice.

3 Cream the butter and sugar. Beat in the treacle, orange rind and vanilla extract.

4 Add the eggs, one at a time, with a little of the flour, beating well after each addition. Fold in the fruit and 30ml/2 tbsp of the whisky. Mix well. Put the mixture into the tin and smooth it down well, making a slight hollow in the centre.

5 Preheat the oven to 160°C/325°F/Gas 3. Bake the cake for 1½ hours, until just beginning to brown. Reduce the heat to 150°C/300°F/Gas 2 and bake for another 3 hours. Cover the top loosely with foil to prevent it from overbrowning.

6 Cool in the tin. Turn upside down, pierce all over with a skewer and pour in the remaining whisky. When it has soaked in, wrap the cake in a double layer of baking parchment followed by foil. Store in an airtight tin in a cool place.

NUTRITIONAL INFORMATION: Energy 9834kcal/41,553kJ; Protein 89.9g; Carbohydrate 1846.1g, of which sugars 1673.2g; Fat 247g, of which saturates 127.3g; Cholesterol 1.39g; Calcium 2.24g; Fibre 46g; Sodium 2.8g.

Yule Log

This rich seasonal treat is a classic alternative to a traditional iced fruit cake.

ingredients

MAKES ONE 28cm/11in
LONG ROLL

- 4 eggs, separated
- 150g/5oz/¾ cup caster (superfine) sugar
- 5ml/1 tsp vanilla extract
- a pinch of cream of tartar
- 115g/4oz/1 cup plain (all-purpose) flour, sifted
- 250ml/8fl oz/1 cup whipping cream
- 300g/11oz plain (semisweet) chocolate, chopped
- 30ml/2 tbsp rum or cognac
- icing (confectioners') sugar, for dusting

1 Preheat the oven to 190°C/ 375°F/Gas 5. Grease and line a 40 x 28cm/16 x 11in Swiss roll tin (jelly roll pan), then dust it lightly with flour.

2 Whisk the egg yolks with all but 25g/1oz/¼ cup of the sugar until pale and thick. Add the vanilla extract.

3 Whisk the egg whites with the cream of tartar until they form soft peaks. Add the reserved sugar and continue whisking until the mixture is stiff and glossy.

4 Fold half the flour into the yolk mixture. Add a quarter of the egg whites and fold in to lighten the mixture. Fold in the remaining flour, then the remaining egg whites.

5 Spread the mixture in the tin. Bake for 15 minutes. Turn out on to paper sprinkled with caster sugar. Roll up and leave to cool.

6 Bring the cream to the boil in a pan. Put the chocolate in a bowl, add the cream and stir until the chocolate has melted. Leave to cool.

7 Whisk the chocolate cream until it is fluffy and thickened to a spreading consistency. Mix one-third of the chocolate cream with the rum or cognac.

8 Unroll the cake and spread with the rum mixture. Re-roll and cut off about a quarter, at an angle. Arrange the smaller piece beside the main roll to represent a branch.

9 Spread the chocolate cream over the cake. Mark the cream with a fork and dust with icing sugar. Add Christmas decorations or a sprig of holly to finish.

NUTRITIONAL INFORMATION: Energy 3826kcal/16020kJ; Protein 56.6g;
Carbohydrate 443.4g, of which sugars 353g; Fat 208.4g, of which saturates 119.9g;
Cholesterol 1042mg; Calcium 599mg; Fibre 11.1g; Sodium 373mg.

Iced Christmas Torte

Not everyone likes traditional Christmas pudding and this is an exciting alternative.

ingredients

SERVES EIGHT TO TEN

- 75g/3oz/¾ cup dried cranberries
- 75g/3oz/scant ½ cup stoned (pitted) prunes
- 50g/2oz/⅓ cup sultanas (golden raisins)
- 175ml/6fl oz/¾ cup port
- 2 pieces preserved stem ginger, finely chopped
- 25g/1oz/2 tbsp unsalted (sweet) butter
- 45ml/3 tbsp light muscovado (brown) sugar
- 90g/3½oz/scant 2 cups fresh white breadcrumbs
- 600ml/1 pint/2½ cups double (heavy) cream
- 30ml/2 tbsp icing (confectioners') sugar
- 5ml/1 tsp ground mixed spice
- 75g/3oz/¾ cup brazil nuts, finely chopped
- sugared bay leaves and fresh cherries, to decorate

1 Put the cranberries, prunes and sultanas in a food processor and process briefly. Tip them into a bowl and add the port and ginger. Leave to absorb the port for 2 hours.

2 Melt the butter in a frying pan. Add the sugar and heat gently until the sugar has dissolved. Tip in the breadcrumbs and stir lightly, then fry over a low heat for about 5 minutes or until lightly coloured and turning crisp. Remove from the heat and leave to cool.

3 Process the breadcrumbs in a food processor or blender until fine. Sprinkle a third into an 18cm/7in loose-based springform tin (pan) and freeze.

4 Whip the cream with the icing sugar and spice until thick but not in peaks. Fold in the brazil nuts and fruit mixture with any unabsorbed port.

5 Spread a third of the mixture over the crumbs, keeping them in place. Top with more layers of crumbs and cream, ending with cream. Freeze overnight.

6 To make sugared bay leaves, dampen the leaves and dust them generously with caster sugar, then leave to dry. Soften the torte in the refrigerator for about 1 hour before serving. Decorate with sugared bay leaves and cherries.

NUTRITIONAL INFORMATION: Energy 504kcal/2098kJ; Protein 6.3g; Carbohydrate 38.4g, of which sugars 21g; Fat 36.4g, of which saturates 17.8g; Cholesterol 61mg; Calcium 92mg; Fibre 2.3g; Sodium 209mg

Christmas Panettone

This classic Italian bread is surprisingly light even though it is rich with butter and dried fruit.

ingredients

MAKES ONE LOAF

- 400g/14oz/3½ cups unbleached white bread flour, plus extra
- 2.5ml/½ tsp salt
- 15g/½ oz fresh yeast
- 120ml/4fl oz/½ cup lukewarm milk
- 2 eggs plus 2 egg yolks
- 75g/3oz/6 tbsp caster (superfine) sugar
- 150g/5oz/⅔ cup unsalted (sweet) butter, softened
- 115g/4oz/⅔ cup mixed chopped (candied) peel
- 75g/3oz/½ cup raisins
- melted butter, for brushing

1 Line and butter a 15cm/6in deep cake tin (pan). Use double-thick paper and cut it 7.5cm/3in above the tin's rim.

2 Sift the flour and salt into a bowl. Make a well in the centre. Cream the yeast with a little of the milk, then mix in the rest.

3 Pour the yeast into the centre of the flour, add the whole eggs and mix in enough flour to make a thick batter. Sprinkle a little of the remaining flour over the liquid and leave in a warm place, for 30 minutes.

4 Add the egg yolks and sugar and mix to a soft dough. Work in the softened butter. Turn the dough out on to a lightly floured surface and knead for 5 minutes until smooth and elastic.

5 Place in a lightly oiled bowl, cover with lightly oiled clear film (plastic wrap) and leave to rise, in a warm place, for 2 hours, or until doubled in bulk.

6 Knock back (punch down) the dough and turn out on to a lightly floured surface. Gently knead in the peel and raisins.

7 Shape the dough into a ball and place in the tin. Cover and leave to rise as before for about 1 hour, or until doubled in size.

8 Preheat the oven to 190°C/375°F/Gas 5. Brush the bread with melted butter and cut a cross in the top.

9 Bake for 20 minutes, then reduce the oven temperature to 180°C/350°F/Gas 4. Brush with butter again and bake for 25 minutes, or until golden. Cool slightly in the tin, then turn out on to a wire rack.

NUTRITIONAL INFORMATION: Energy 3599kcal/15123kJ; Protein 65.7g; Carbohydrate 515.7g, of which sugars 210.9g; Fat 156.2g, of which saturates 87.1g; Cholesterol 1187mg; Calcium 1070mg; Fibre 19.4g; Sodium 1530mg.

Greek New Year Cake

A foil-wrapped gold coin is traditionally baked into this almond and sesame cake.

ingredients

MAKES ONE 23cm/9in
SQUARE CAKE

- 275g/10oz/2½ cups plain (all-purpose) flour
- 10ml/2 tsp baking powder
- 50g/2oz/½ cup ground almonds
- 225g/8oz/1 cup butter
- 175g/6oz/generous ¾ cup caster (superfine) sugar, plus extra for sprinkling
- 4 eggs
- 150ml/¼ pint/⅔ cup fresh orange juice
- 50g/2oz/½ cup blanched almonds
- 15g/½ oz/1 tbsp sesame seeds

1 Preheat the oven to 180°C/350°F/Gas 4. Grease a 23cm/9in square cake tin (pan), line with baking parchment and grease the paper.

2 Sift together the flour and baking powder and stir in the ground almonds.

3 Cream the butter and sugar until light and fluffy. Beat in the eggs, one at a time. Fold in the flour mixture, alternating with the orange juice. Spoon the mixture into the prepared cake tin.

4 Arrange the blanched almonds on top of the cake in pairs. Sprinkle over the sesame seeds.

5 Bake for about 50 minutes, or until a skewer inserted into the centre of the cake comes out clean.

6 Leave the cake in the tin for 5 minutes. Then turn it out on to a wire rack, peel off the lining paper and leave to cool. Sprinkle the top of the cake with caster sugar before serving.

cook's tip

Do not overbeat the mixture – this will cause the cake to sag in the middle. Scrape the mixture from the sides of the bowl as you mix so that all the ingredients are incorporated.

NUTRITIONAL INFORMATION: Energy 4261kcal/17800kJ; Protein 74.9g; Carbohydrate 418g, of which sugars 205.7g; Fat 266.7g, of which saturates 128.4g; Cholesterol 1241mg; Calcium 887mg; Fibre 16.1g; Sodium 1091mg.

Easter Kulich

This rich Russian yeast cake is traditionally made at Eastertime.

ingredients

MAKES TWO CAKES

- 15ml/1 tbsp active dried yeast
- 90ml/6 tbsp lukewarm milk
- 75g/3oz/6 tbsp caster (superfine) sugar
- 500g/1¼ lb/5 cups plain (all-purpose) flour
- a pinch of saffron threads
- 30ml/2 tbsp dark rum
- 2.5ml/½ tsp ground cardamom seeds
- 2.5ml/½ tsp ground cumin
- 50g/2oz/¼ cup unsalted (sweet) butter
- 2 eggs plus 2 egg yolks
- ½ vanilla pod (bean), finely chopped
- 25g/1oz/2 tbsp each crystallized ginger, mixed (candied) peel, almonds and currants, chopped

For the decoration

- 75g/3oz/¾ cup icing (confectioners') sugar, sifted
- 7.5–10ml/1½–2 tsp warm water
- drop of almond extract
- blanched almonds
- mixed (candied) peel
- 1 candle

1 Blend together the yeast, milk, 25g/1oz/¼ cup sugar and 50g/2oz/½ cup flour. Leave in a warm place for 15 minutes, or until frothy. Soak the saffron in the rum for 15 minutes.

2 Sift together the remaining flour and spices and rub in the butter. Stir in the rest of the sugar. Add the yeast mixture, saffron liquid and remaining ingredients. Knead the dough until smooth. Put in an oiled bowl, cover with clear film (plastic wrap) and leave until doubled in size.

3 Preheat the oven to 190°C/375°F/Gas 5. Line, grease and flour two 500g/1¼lb coffee tins or 15cm/6in clay flowerpots.

4 Knock back (punch down) the dough. Shape into two rounds, place in tins or pots, cover and prove for 30 minutes. Bake for 35 minutes for pots or 50 minutes for tins. Cool on a wire rack.

5 For the icing, mix the icing sugar, water and almond extract. Pour over the cakes and decorate with almonds, mixed peel and the candle.

NUTRITIONAL INFORMATION: Energy 1521kcal/6432kJ; Protein 33.3g; Carbohydrate 282.3g, of which sugars 91.8g; Fat 33g, of which saturates 16.4g; Cholesterol 347mg; Calcium 505mg; Fibre 8.4g; Sodium 293mg.

Easter Simnel Cake

This cake dates back to medieval times, and is traditionally served at Easter or on Mothering Sunday.

ingredients

MAKES ONE 18cm/7in ROUND CAKE

- 175g/6oz/¾ cup unsalted (sweet) butter
- 175g/6oz/scant 1 cup soft brown sugar
- 3 large eggs, beaten
- 225g/8oz/2 cups plain (all-purpose) flour
- 2.5ml/½ tsp ground cinnamon
- 2.5ml/½ tsp nutmeg, grated
- 150g/5oz/1 cup each of currants, sultanas (golden raisins) and raisins
- 85g/3oz/generous ½ cup glacé (candied) cherries, quartered
- 85g/3oz/generous ½ cup mixed (candied) peel, chopped
- grated rind of 1 large lemon
- 450g/1lb almond paste
- 1 egg white, lightly beaten

1 Line and grease an 18cm/7in round tin (pan). Tie double-thick brown paper round the outside.

2 Beat the butter and sugar until pale and fluffy, then gradually beat in the eggs. Lightly fold in the flour, spices, dried fruits, cherries, mixed peel and lemon rind.

3 Preheat the oven to 160°C/325°F/Gas 3. Roll out half the almond paste into a 16cm/6½in circle on a surface lightly dusted with caster sugar.

4 Spoon half the cake mixture into the prepared tin and place the circle of almond paste on top. Spoon the remaining cake mixture on top, spreading evenly and levelling the surface.

5 Bake for 1 hour. Reduce the oven temperature to 150°C/300°F/Gas 2 and cook for another 2 hours. If the top begins to brown too quickly, cover loosely with a piece of foil.

6 Leave to cool for 1 hour in the tin, then turn out and cool on a wire rack.

7 Brush the cake with egg white. Roll out half the remaining almond paste to a 28cm/11in circle and place this on top of the cake. Roll the remaining paste into 11 balls and attach them to the top of the cake with egg white. Brush the top of the cake with more egg white and grill (broil) until lightly browned.

NUTRITIONAL INFORMATION: Energy 8108kcal/34162kJ; Protein 104g; Carbohydrate 1323.3g, of which sugars 1113.8g; Fat 303.9g, of which saturates 132.5g; Cholesterol 1442mg; Calcium 1557mg; Fibre 33.4g; Sodium 2080mg.

Basketweave Wedding Cake

This fabulous cake is iced using a simple yet effective basketweave technique.

ingredients

SERVES 150

- 25cm/10in, 20cm/8in and 15cm/6in square Madeira cakes (see p1 for recipe)
- 2.75kg/6lb/12 cups butter icing

Materials/equipment

- 30cm/12in square silver cake board
- 20cm/8in and 15cm/6in thin silver cake board
- smooth scraper
- 12 small baking parchment piping (icing) bags
- medium writing and basketweave nozzles
- 1.5m/1½yd pale lilac ribbon, 2.5cm/1in wide
- 2.5m/2½yd deep lilac ribbon, 5mm/¼in wide
- 30 fresh lilac-coloured freesias

1 Level the cake tops, then invert the cakes on to the boards and cover with butter icing. Use a smooth scraper on the sides and a metal spatula to smooth the top. Leave to set for 1 hour.

cook's tip

To make 350g/12oz/1½ cups butter icing, beat 75g/3oz/ 6 tbsp butter with 225g/8oz/ 2 cups icing (confectioners') sugar and 10ml/2 tsp milk until light and fluffy.

2 Pipe a line of icing with the medium writing nozzle on to the corner of the large cake, from the base to the top.

3 Using the basketweave nozzle, pipe a basketweave pattern around the side of the cake. Neaten the top edge with a shell border, using the same nozzle. Repeat for the second cake.

4 To decorate the top of the small cake, start at the edge with a straight plain line, then pipe across with the basketweave nozzle, spacing the lines equally.

5 When the top is complete, work the design around the sides, making sure the design aligns on the top and sides. Leave the cakes overnight to set.

6 Fit the wide ribbon around the board, then the narrow ribbon on top. Tie eight small bows with the remaining ribbon. Assemble the cakes, then decorate with the bows and the flowers.

NUTRITIONAL INFORMATION: Energy 180kcal/754kJ; Protein 1.5g; Carbohydrate 26.1g, of which sugars 20.2g; Fat 8.4g, of which saturates 5g; Cholesterol 11mg; Calcium 17mg; Fibre 0.2g; Sodium 134mg.

Lucky Horseshoe Cake

This horseshoe-shaped cake is cut from a round cake – it's a good shape for all occasions.

ingredients

MAKES ONE 25cm/10in
HORSESHOE CAKE

- 25cm/10in rich fruit cake (see
  p7 for recipe)
- 60ml/4 tbsp apricot jam,
  warmed and sieved (strained)
- 800g/1¾lb marzipan
- 1kg/2¼lb/7½ cups
  sugarpaste icing
- peach and blue food colourings
- edible silver balls
- 115g/4oz/¾ cup royal icing

Materials/equipment

- 30cm/12in round cake board
- crimping tool
- blue ribbon, 3mm/⅛in wide
- large and small blossom cutters

1 Make a horseshoe template and use to cut the cake. Brush the cake with the apricot jam. Roll out 350g/12oz of the marzipan to a 25cm/10in circle. Using the template, cut out the shape and place on the cake.

2 Measure the side of the cake. Roll and cut out a strip from the remaining marzipan and use to cover the side. Place the cake on the board and leave overnight. Tint 800g/1¾lb/5¼ cups of the sugarpaste peach. Cover the cake as before. Crimp the top edge.

3 Draw and measure the ribbon insertion for the top of the cake on the template. Cut 13 pieces of ribbon fractionally longer than each slit. Make the slits through the template on the cake using a scalpel. Insert the pieces of ribbon with a cocktail stick (toothpick). Leave to dry overnight.

cook's tip

Sugarpaste icing and royal icing can be bought ready-made from most supermarkets.

4 Make a tiny horseshoe template. Tint half the remaining sugarpaste icing blue. Using the template, cut out nine blue shapes. Mark each horseshoe with a sharp knife.

5 Using the blossom cutters, cut out 12 large and 15 small flower shapes. Press a silver ball into the centre of the larger shapes. Repeat with the white icing.

6 Decorate the cake with the blossoms, ribbon and horseshoes, securing with dots of white royal icing.

NUTRITIONAL INFORMATION: Energy 8428kcal/35700kJ; Protein 73.6g; Carbohydrate 1733g, of which sugars 1654.6g; Fat 159g, of which saturates 25g; Cholesterol 323mg; Calcium 1459mg; Fibre 25.7g; Sodium 1304mg.

Halloween Ghost Cake

This children's cake is really simple to make yet very effective. It is ideal for a Halloween party.

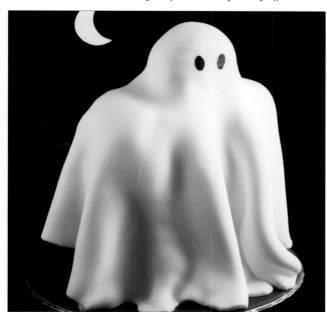

ingredients

SERVES FIFTEEN TO TWENTY

- 900g/2lb/6½ cups white sugarpaste icing
- black food colouring
- 2 Madeira cakes, baked in an 18cm/7in square cake tin and a 300ml/½ pint/1¼ cup round bowl (see p1 for recipe)
- 350g/12oz/1½ cups butter icing (see p93 for recipe)

Materials/equipment

- 23cm/9in round cake board
- fine paintbrush

1 Tint 115g/4oz/¾ cup of the sugarpaste icing dark grey and use it to cover the cake board.

2 Cut two small corners off the large square cake. Cut two larger wedges off the other two corners.

3 Stand the cake on the board and secure with a little butter icing. Divide the larger trimmings in half and wedge them around the base of the cake.

4 Secure the small cake to the top of the larger cake with butter icing.

cook's tip

Instead of painting on the eyes, you could colour some sugarpaste trimmings black and cut out two oval shapes.

5 Completely cover both of the cakes with the remaining butter icing. Roll out the remaining sugarpaste icing to an oval 50 x 30cm/20 x 12in. Lay the icing over the cake, gently dropping it into folds around the sides.

6 Smooth the icing over the top half of the cake. Trim off excess sugarpaste that overhangs the board. Using a fine paintbrush, paint two eyes with black food colouring.

NUTRITIONAL INFORMATION: Energy 344kcal/1447kJ; Protein 2.6g; Carbohydrate 57.7g, of which sugars 47.8g; Fat 13g, of which saturates 7.7g; Cholesterol 16mg; Calcium 36mg; Fibre 0.4g; Sodium 218mg.

Cloth-of-roses Cake

This lovely cake simply says "congratulations". It is pretty and bound to impress guests.

ingredients

MAKES ONE 20cm/8in
ROUND CAKE

- 20cm/8in round fruit cake (see p7 for recipe)
- 45ml/3 tbsp apricot jam, warmed and sieved (strained)
- 675g/1½lb marzipan
- 900g/2lb/6½ cups sugarpaste icing
- yellow, orange and green food colourings
- 115g/4oz/¾ cup royal icing

Materials/equipment

- 25cm/10in cake board
- 5.5cm/2¼in plain cutter
- thin yellow ribbon

1 Brush the cake all over with apricot jam. Cover with marzipan, trim and leave to dry overnight.

2 Cut off 675g/1½lb/4½ cups of the sugarpaste icing and divide in half. Colour pale yellow and pale orange.

3 Make a baking parchment template for the orange icing. Draw a circle round the cake board. Using the plain cutter, draw scallops around the outside. Cover the side of the cake with yellow sugarpaste icing. Place on the board.

4 Using the template, cut out the orange icing. Place it on the top of the cake, bending the edges slightly. Leave overnight.

5 Cut off three-quarters of the remaining sugarpaste icing and divide into four.

6 Tint the icing different shades of yellow and orange. Make 18 roses by making a cone, then flattening five balls of paste and attaching them to the cone.

7 Tint the remaining icing green and cut out 24 leaves. Secure the leaves and roses with royal icing. Add the ribbon.

NUTRITIONAL INFORMATION: Energy 8469kcal/35840kJ; Protein 80.3g; Carbohydrate 1682.1g, of which sugars 1563.6g; Fat 204.1g, of which saturates 62.1g; Cholesterol 0mg; Calcium 1302mg; Fibre 12.8g; Sodium 2130mg.

Flickering Birthday Candle Cake

Flickering stripy candles are ready to blow out on this birthday cake for all ages.

ingredients

MAKES ONE 20cm/8in
SQUARE CAKE

- 20cm/8in square Madeira cake (see p1 for recipe)
- 350g/12oz/1½ cups butter icing (see p93 for recipe)
- 45ml/3 tbsp apricot jam, warmed and sieved (strained)
- 800g/1¾lb/5¼ cups sugarpaste icing
- pink, yellow, purple and jade food colourings
- edible silver balls

Materials/equipment

- 23cm/9in square cake board
- small round cutter
- pink and purple food colouring pens
- 5mm/¼ in-wide jade-coloured ribbon

1 Slice the cake horizontally into three layers. Sandwich the layers back together with the butter icing. Brush off any loose crumbs from the cake and then brush it lightly all over with the apricot jam.

2 Roll out 500g/1¼lb/3¾ cups of the sugarpaste icing and use to cover the cake. Position on the cake board.

3 Divide the remaining sugarpaste into four pieces and tint them pink, yellow, pale purple and jade.

4 Make the candles from jade and the flames from yellow icing, rolling it out evenly and cutting the strips and petal shapes for the flames. Press a silver ball into their bases. Position the candles and flames on the cake with a little water. Mould strips in yellow and purple icing to go around the candles. Secure with water.

5 Cut out the small wavy pieces from the pink and purple icing to represent a glow and smoke, and arrange them, using water, above the candles.

6 Cut out yellow circles with the cutter for the side decorations. Mould small pink balls and press a silver ball into their centres. Attach using water.

7 Using food colouring pens, draw wavy lines and dots coming from the purple and pink wavy icings. Decorate the sides of the cake board with the ribbon, securing at the back with a small piece of softened sugarpaste.

NUTRITIONAL INFORMATION: Energy 6841kcal/28896kJ; Protein 45.4g; Carbohydrate 1305.7g, of which sugars 1141.4g; Fat 195.4g, of which saturates 115.3g; Cholesterol 213mg; Calcium 762mg; Fibre 6.8g; Sodium 3517mg.

Gift-wrapped Parcel

If you don't have a tiny flower cutter for this design, then press a small button into the soft icing.

ingredients

MAKES ONE 15cm/6in
SQUARE CAKE

- 15cm/6in square cake
- 50g/2oz/4 tbsp butter icing
  (see p93 for recipe)
- 45ml/3 tbsp apricot jam,
  warmed and sieved (strained)
- 450g/1lb marzipan
- 350g/12oz/2¼ cups pale
  lemon yellow sugarpaste icing
- red and green food colourings
- 30ml/2 tbsp royal icing

Materials/equipment

- 20cm/8in square cake board
- small flower cutter (optional)

1 Split the cake and fill with butter icing. Place on the cake board and brush with the warmed apricot jam.

2 Cover with half the marzipan, then with the yellow sugarpaste icing, and mark with a small flower cutter.

3 To make the ribbons, divide the remaining marzipan in half, and colour one half pink and the other pale green. Roll out the pink marzipan and cut into four 2.5 x 18cm/ 1 x 7in strips.

4 Roll out the green marzipan and cut into four 1 x 18cm/ ¹/₂ x 7in strips. Centre them on top of the pink strips and stick on to the cake with a little water.

5 Cut two 5cm/2in strips from each colour and cut a "V" from the ends to form ribbon. Stick in place and dry overnight.

6 Cut the remaining green into four 2.5 x 7.5cm/1 x 3in lengths and the pink into four 1 x 7.5cm/ ¹/₂ x 3in lengths. Centre the pink on top of the green, fold in half and stick the ends together.

7 Slip the marzipan pieces over the handle of a wooden spoon, dusted with cornflour (cornstarch). Leave overnight.

8 Cut the ends into "V" shapes to fit neatly together on the cake. Cut two pieces for the join in the centre. Remove the bows from the spoon and stick in position with royal icing.

NUTRITIONAL INFORMATION: Energy 5031kcal/21295kJ; Protein 72.6g; Carbohydrate 992g, of which sugars 596g; Fat 116.3g, of which saturates 36g; Cholesterol 107mg; Calcium 442mg; Fibre 8.6g; Sodium 417mg.

Ladybird Cake

Children will love this colourful and appealing ladybird, and it is very simple to make.

ingredients

SERVES TEN TO TWELVE

- 3-egg quantity quick-mix sponge cake
- 175g/6oz/¾ cup butter icing (see p93 for recipe)
- 60ml/4 tbsp lemon curd, warmed
- icing (confectioners') sugar, for dusting
- 1kg/2¼lb/6¾ cup sugarpaste icing
- red, black and green food colourings

Materials/equipment

- 23cm/9in square cake board
- 2 pipe cleaners, coloured black

1 Preheat the oven to 180°C/350°F/Gas 4. Grease and line the base of a 1.2 litre/2 pint/5 cup ovenproof bowl. Spoon in the cake mixture and smooth the surface. Bake for 55–60 minutes, or until a skewer inserted into the centre comes out clean. Cool.

2 Cut the cake in half crossways and sandwich together with the butter icing. Cut vertically through the cake, about a third of the way in. Brush both pieces with the lemon curd.

3 Colour 450g/1lb/3 cups of the sugarpaste icing red. Dust a work surface with icing sugar and roll out the icing to about 5mm/¼in thick. Use to cover the larger piece of cake to make the body. Using a wooden skewer, make an indentation down the centre for the wings.

4 Colour 350g/12oz/2¼ cups of the sugarpaste icing black, roll out three-quarters and use to cover the smaller piece of cake for the head. Place both cakes on the cake board and press them together in place.

5 Roll out 50g/2oz/⅓ cup icing. Cut out two 5cm/2in white circles for the eyes. Stick to the head with water. Roll out the remaining black icing and cut out eight 4cm/1½in circles: use two of these for the eyes and stick the others on to the body.

6 Colour some icing green and squeeze through a garlic press to make the grass.

7 Press a ball of black icing on to the end of each pipe cleaner for the feelers. Arrange the grass on the board around the cake.

NUTRITIONAL INFORMATION: Energy 539kcal/2270kJ; Protein 3.8g; Carbohydrate 92.7g, of which sugars 80.2g; Fat 19.5g, of which saturates 6.3g; Cholesterol 70mg; Calcium 69mg; Fibre 0.5g; Sodium 209mg.

Frog Prince Cake

Our happy frog will bring a smile to any young child's face – and will probably even get a kiss!

ingredients

SERVES EIGHT TO TEN
- 20cm/8in round sponge cake (see p2 for recipe)
- 115g/4oz/1/2 cup butter icing (see p93 for recipe)
- 45ml/3 tbsp apricot jam, warmed and sieved (strained)
- 450g/1lb marzipan
- 500g/1 1/4 lb/3 3/4 cups sugarpaste icing
- 115g/4oz/3/4 cup royal icing
- green, red, black and gold food colourings

Materials/equipment
- 25cm/10in square cake board
- glass
- fine paintbrush

1 Split the cake and fill with butter icing. Cut in half and sandwich the halves with apricot jam. Stand the cake on end across the board. Brush with jam and cover with marzipan.

2 Tint 450g/1lb/3 cups of the sugarpaste green and cover the cake. Roll the remaining green into 1cm/1/2in diameter sausages. Use two folded 20cm/8in lengths for back legs and 14 x 10cm/4in lengths for front legs and feet. Stick with royal icing. Roll balls for eyes and stick in place.

3 For the crown, roll out the reserved sugarpaste icing and cut a 5 x 19cm/2 x 7 1/2 in strip. Cut out triangles along one edge to make the crown shape. Wrap this around a glass dusted with cornflour (cornstarch) and moisten the edges to join them firmly together. Leave the crown to dry until firm.

4 Cut a 10cm/4in circle for the white shirt. Stick this in place on the front of the frog and trim the base edge neatly. Cut white circles and stick them in place for the eyes.

5 Tint a little sugarpaste pink, roll into a sausage and stick on for the mouth. Tint the rest black and use for the pupils and the bow tie. Stick in place.

6 Paint the crown with gold food colouring, leave to dry, then stick into position with a little royal icing.

cook's tip

You could write the frog's name on the front of his shirt; or write Happy Birthday here.

NUTRITIONAL INFORMATION: Energy 681kcal/2862kJ; Protein 7g; Carbohydrate 104.7g, of which sugars 89.3g; Fat 28.9g, of which saturates 7.1g; Cholesterol 89mg; Calcium 97mg; Fibre 1.5g; Sodium 271mg.

Noah's Ark Cake

This charming cake is decorated with small animals available from cake decorating stores.

ingredients

MAKES ONE 20 x 13cm/
8 x 5in CAKE

- 20cm/8in square sponge cake (see p2 for recipe)
- 115g/4oz/½ cup butter icing (see p93 for recipe)
- 45ml/3 tbsp apricot jam, warmed and sieved (strained)
- 450g/1lb marzipan
- 450g/1lb/3 cups sugarpaste icing
- brown, yellow and blue food colourings
- 115g/4oz/¾ cup royal icing
- chocolate mint stick

Materials/equipment

- 25cm/10in square cake board
- skewer
- rice paper
- small animal cake ornaments

1 Split the cake and sandwich it back together with a little butter icing. Cut off and set aside a 7.5cm/3in strip of cake. Shape the remaining piece of cake to form the hull of the boat. Place this diagonally on the cake board.

2 Use the set-aside piece of cake to cut a rectangle 10 x 6cm/4 x 2½in for the cabin and a triangular piece for the roof of the ark. Sandwich the roof and the cabin together with a little butter icing or apricot jam.

3 Cover the three pieces with a layer of marzipan. Tint the sugarpaste brown and use most of it to cover the hull and cabin.

4 Use the remaining brown icing to make a long sausage. Stick around the edge of the hull with water. Mark planks with the back of a knife. Leave to dry overnight.

5 Tint one-third of the royal icing yellow and spread it over the cabin roof with a metal spatula. Roughen it with a skewer to create a thatch.

6 Tint the remaining royal icing blue and spread over the cake board, making rough waves.

7 Cut a small triangle out of rice paper to make a flag. Stick the flag on to the chocolate mint stick and press on the back of the boat.

8 Stick each of the small animal ornaments on to the boat with a dab of royal icing.

NUTRITIONAL INFORMATION: Energy 6888kcal/28960kJ; Protein 70.3g; Carbohydrate 1068.1g, of which sugars 914.1g; Fat 288.6g, of which saturates 71.3g; Cholesterol 890mg; Calcium 980mg; Fibre 14.9g; Sodium 2709mg.

COOK'S NOTES

Bracketed terms are intended for American readers.

For all recipes, quantities are given in both metric and imperial measures and, where appropriate, in standard cups and spoons. Follow one set of measures, but not a mixture, because they are not interchangeable.

Standard spoon and cup measures are level. 1 tsp = 5ml, 1 tbsp = 15ml, 1 cup = 250ml/8fl oz.

Australian standard tablespoons are 20ml. Australian readers should use 3 tsp in place of 1 tbsp for measuring small quantities.

American pints are 16fl oz/2 cups. American readers should use 20fl oz/2.5 cups in place of 1 pint when measuring liquids.

Electric oven temperatures in this book are for conventional ovens. When using a fan oven, the temperature will probably need to be reduced by about 10–20°C/20–40°F. Since ovens vary, you should check with your manufacturer's instruction book for guidance.

The nutritional analysis given for each recipe is calculated per portion (i.e. serving or item), unless otherwise stated. If the recipe gives a range, such as Serves 4–6, then the nutritional analysis will be for the smaller portion size, i.e. 6 servings. Measurements for sodium do not include salt added to taste.

Medium (US large) eggs are used unless otherwise stated.

This edition is published by Lorenz Books, an imprint of Anness Publishing Ltd, Blaby Road, Wigston, Leicestershire LE18 4SE; info@anness.com

www.lorenzbooks.com; www.annesspublishing.com

If you like the images in this book and would like to investigate using them for publishing, promotions or advertising, please visit our website www.practicalpictures.com for more information.

© Anness Publishing Ltd 2012

A CIP catalogue record for this book is available from the British Library.